CW01164246

West & South West London
Edited by Annabel Cook & Mark Richardson

First published in Great Britain in 2007 by:
Young Writers
Remus House
Coltsfoot Drive
Peterborough
PE2 9JX
Telephone: 01733 890066
Website: www.youngwriters.co.uk

All Rights Reserved

© Copyright Contributors 2007

SB ISBN 978-1 84431 287 0

Foreword

Young Writers was established in 1991 and has been passionately devoted to the promotion of reading and writing in children and young adults ever since. The quest continues today. Young Writers remains as committed to the nurturing of poetic and literary talent as ever.

This year's Young Writers competition has proven as vibrant and dynamic as ever and we are delighted to present a showcase of the best poetry from across the UK and in some cases overseas. Each poem has been selected from a wealth of *Little Laureates* entries before ultimately being published in this, our sixteenth primary school poetry series.

Once again, we have been supremely impressed by the overall quality of the entries we have received. The imagination, energy and creativity which has gone into each young writer's entry made choosing the poems a challenging and often difficult but ultimately hugely rewarding task - the general high standard of the work submitted ensured this opportunity to bring their poetry to a larger appreciative audience.

We sincerely hope you are pleased with this final collection and that you will enjoy *Little Laureates West & South West London* for many years to come.

Contents

Albermarle Primary School, Wimbledon
Kayinaat Asif (10)	1
Kirsty Clarke (10)	1
Josie Allen (9)	2
Tom O'Shea	2
Darius Elliott (10)	3
Iman El-Bouzidi (9)	3
Ellesse Abbott (9)	4
Amy Risley (10)	5
Jasmin Chopra (10)	6
Chloe Adams (9)	7
Rasharn Gabbidon-McLean (9)	8

Avonmore Primary School, West Kensington
Mica Merid (8)	8
William Taylor (10)	9
Savera Khalid (9)	9
Armaghan Hallajian (10)	10
Georgina Riley (9)	11
Eleanor Matthews (9)	12
Ammar Roomi (9)	12
Elliott Campbell (9)	13
Zahra Hussien (9)	13
Yllka Fejzullahu (10)	14
Chloe Hillier (10)	15
Jasmine Momeni (10)	15
Charlotte Evans (8)	16
Julia Glotova (9)	16
Onyinyechi Okorie (8)	17
Ned Prevezer (8)	17
Darnell Tetteh (8)	18
Thubelihle Mguni (8)	18
Alice Center (8)	19
Eve Staheli (9)	19
Noor Zaini (8)	20
Jennifer Bazilyuk (9)	20
Finlay Watson (7)	21
Dhuha Sajjad (9)	22
Saffa Abdi (8)	22

Alice Armstrong (9) — 23
Omar Harb (9) — 23
Aya Saleh (9) — 24
Samuel Apaijitt (7) — 24
Duff Westmoreland (10) — 25
Kate Bazilyuk (9) — 25
Maya Harnady (10) — 26
Andy Tarshalla (9) — 26
Phoebe Watts (10) — 27
Olivia Traverso Madden (9) — 28
Marwa Abdi (8) — 28

Eardley Primary School, Streatham
Rachael Kingsley (10) — 29
Hebe Perry-Belfrage (10) — 29
Berthram Silvera (11) — 29
Tierney Glide (11) — 30
Fanxi Liu (8) — 30
Tamicha Rochester-Prosper (10) — 31
Zandria Vas (10) — 31
Marisa, Janna & Daniele (11) — 32
Nneka Williams (10) — 32
Esosa Uwaifo (11) — 32
Corey Nurse (10) — 33
Hassan Mahmud (11) — 33
Luke Lacriarde (10) — 33
Fatima Sunni (9) — 34
Mohamed Aden (11) — 34
Jhelisa Graham (11) — 35
Sebastian Sandhir (10) — 35
Terentino Mills & Kofi Amaadzie (10) — 36
Sabrina Rafiq (11) — 37
Akhirah Hulcome (11) — 37
Tyler Moore (11) — 38
Yonis Nur (11) — 38
Teeyana Graham (10) — 38
Maya Sharda (8) — 39
Aaron Matteus-Hendricks (11) — 39
Layla Dhiman (8) — 39
Quinn Mireku (8) — 40
Zaiba Nadeem (8) — 40

Lily Dovey-Linke (8)	41
Ephraim Conteh (8)	41
Sakina Kashmiri (10)	41
Samirah Oyede (9)	42
David Wan (11)	42
Clare Stringer (8)	43
Renee Guisle (9)	43
Jazzim Saroochi (10)	44
Fahd Arif (12)	44
Ella Rimmer (10)	45
Khalil Lafta (11)	45
Charesia Patten (11)	46
Yuyi Kabanje & Romello Armani-Cozier (11)	46
Lareb Naseem (11)	46
Rebecca Thompson (11)	47
Jade Mitchell (8)	47
Chinyere Logan (11)	48
William Duncan Dennis-Hoare (10)	48
Pooja Vara (10)	49
Danial Khan (10)	49

Loughborough Primary School, Brixton

Ruka Yussuff (10)	50
Loretta Yussuff	50
Veneisha Seymour (10)	50
Ridwan Jamir (8)	51
Siobhan Charles (8)	51
Abdi Mohamed (9)	51
Esther Olowu (9)	52
Shanieke Scott (8)	52
Evelyn-Chipo-Mariott-Makuka (9)	52
Ashley McGibbon (9)	53
Sherifah Abdul (8)	53
Emmanuel Smith (8)	53
Leon McClancy (7)	54
Tyler Fraser	54
Chloe McGovern (7)	55
Zhané Smith (10)	55
Olayiwola Amire (10)	56
Ben Breach (10)	56
Britney Piggott (11)	57

Andrew Breach (11)	57
Nataskie Wright (9)	58
Sawida Bedor-Bangura (10)	58
Sergen Etam (10)	59
Reece Gayle (10)	59
Jahmarley Gibson	59
Roqeeb Ajibola (11)	60
Samuel Clayton	60
Ryan Elliott (8)	60
Tian Wallace (10)	61
Kwadwo A Kyei (11)	62
Kane Nosworthy (11)	63
Michael Rodrigues (9)	64
Hayley Gale	64
Conard Haye (8)	64
Mariama Seydou (8)	65
Stephanie Homawoo	65
Diana Yusuf (8)	65
Dayana Herrera Rodriguez (10)	66
Rikaya Johnson	66
Mohammed Bouadina (9)	66
Hamza Arif (8)	67
Ammar Akram (8)	67
Rashad Johnson (10)	68
Sean Brown (10)	68
Layla Habarek (10)	69
Amani Alam (10)	70

Penwortham Primary School, Streatham

Amy Hilton-Banks (9)	70
Ansha Mootoo (10)	71
Lucy Gregory (9)	72
Georgia Field (9)	72
Maia Forde (8)	73
Bethany Monk-Lane (10)	73
Hope Ferary (8)	74
Shakira Reece (10)	74
Max Weller (8)	74
Tayeba Ahmed (10)	75
Rose Eaglesfield (10)	75
Sèverine Howell-Meri (8)	76

Rachael Maybury (9)	76
Matilda Botsford (9)	77
Zoe Forester (9)	77
Ethan Sampson (8)	77
Hope James (9)	78
Jiraporn Mcgill (9)	78
Jordan Hadfield (9)	78
Elliot Winspear (8)	79
Panayiotis Koushi (9)	79
Chloe Corne (10)	80
Antalia Delgado (9)	80
Grace Thomas (9)	81
Jules Bleckman (9)	81
Jake Seymour (10)	82
Sophie Fox (9)	82
Natalie Maybury (9)	82
Ben Bhogal (10)	83
Chelsea Garwood (10)	83
Zainab Malik (9)	84
Nadia Ahmed (10)	84
Riyaaz Patel (10)	85
Uzayr Subratty (9)	85
Ammara Khan (10)	86
Aisling Towl (10)	86
Hamza Mahmood (9)	87
Alice Edmundson (9)	87
Megan Barratt (10)	88
Hasan Gaffar (10)	88

Robin Hood Primary School, Kingston Upon Thames

Alana Emery (8)	88
Dyna Tlemsani (11)	89
Natalia Goncalves (11)	89
Amber Pearce-Debono (10)	90
Nikki Whitby (11)	90
Nathan Richardson (11)	91
Bonnie Maclaren (11)	91
Daniel Knowles (11)	92
Alexandra Jellye (10)	92
Zan Mahmood (10)	93
Craig Norris (10)	93

Sunny Ratilal (10)	94
Carl Mayes (10)	94
Reece Xavier (8)	95
Zaynab Osman (8)	95
Kane Corby (8)	95
Britney Reilly (7)	95
Justin Le (8)	96
Nathanael Taylor (8)	96
Erin Ailes (8)	96
Hassan Mustafa (8)	96
Tommy Iqbal (10)	97
Nora Hakim (9)	97
Antonella Posteraro (10)	97
Daniel McQue (10)	98
Joshua Davis (10)	98
Fatima Hussien (9)	98
Mollie Cummings (9)	98
Isla Paterson (9)	99
Eloise Emery (10)	99
Amber Russell (9)	100
Alana Blackwell-Barnett (7)	100
Rebekah Smith (7)	100
Andrew O'Neill (11)	101
Naomi Arkaah (10)	101
Ali Mustafa (10)	102
Sharif Dougramaji (10)	102
Ellie Macnamara (11)	103
Isabel Slatter (10)	103
Dominique Campbell (8)	104

St Joseph's RC Primary School, Chelsea

Daniel Spinola (10)	104
Mia Dalimot (8)	105
Paula Vilelas (9)	105
Daniela Santos (9)	106
Anais Espinosa (8)	106
Julio Mendes Santos (8)	106
Samuel Makanjuola (10)	107
Dion Galligan (10)	108
Lorena Perez (9)	108
Anthony Oliveira (10)	108

Martin Alban (10)	109
Rosie Bennett (9)	109
Serena Tavares Firmino (10)	110
William Ruales (9)	110
Kari-Ann De Sa Da Silva (10)	111
Adriana Camacho (10)	111
Alana Barker-Perez (10)	112
Alison Martinez (10)	112
Leon Xavier (10)	112
Rania Habib (10)	113
Jasmine De La Cruz (9)	113
Kace Bartley (9)	114
James Poots (10)	115
Fabio Nobrega (9)	115
Jessica Mendes (7)	115
Marina Ayub (9)	116
Daniela Silva (9)	116
Catarina Santos Moreira (9)	117
Lorenzo Benavente (9)	117
Mafalda Ribeiro (8)	118

The Poems

My Mother

My mother is the sweetest most delicate of all,
She knows more of paradise than angels can recall.
She makes me laugh and makes me cry,
But I definitely know that she doesn't lie.

She is my joy and is my sadness,
But sometimes she drives me in madness.
I mumble in my breath when I get really angry,
But after that my tongue goes really tangy.

Here is what it's like:

Mothers same as you,
Sisters sulk,
Brothers blame you,
And dads won't budge until you shov'em,
But they're a family you might as well love them.

Kayinaat Asif (10)
Albermarle Primary School, Wimbledon

My Baby Brother

Roses are red
Violets are blue
My baby brother is so cute
For you.

I feel happen when he's here
It is amazing that my mum was here
My dad is glad that the birth is over
And now we have a beautiful baby brother.

When he gets older I can play with him with my toys
And that will be over.

It is amazing that he is here, now we can move on
And that will be the end of my baby brother and me.

Kirsty Clarke (10)
Albermarle Primary School, Wimbledon

My Dog

Roses are red
Violets are blue
I have a dog
It is called Lady Blue

My dog is a Rottweiler
She is black and golden brown
She likes to play around
And when she wees in the house
It makes my mum frown

She loves to eat her Pedigree treats
She munches them all up
After a long run in the park
She returns home to have a little nap

She plays football in the house with me
We have loads of fun together
I love my little Lady Blue
And I never want her to leave!

Josie Allen (9)
Albermarle Primary School, Wimbledon

I Love My Mum

Love is the colour of flames,
Love is the sound of lovely birds singing in the tree,
Love is like chocolate,
Sweet like apples,
My mum gives me kisses and I like it.

Red as roses like your hair,
I love my mum and she loves me,
My mum is sweet; I admit I love her,
Valentine time is 'I love you' time,
I love my mum and she loves me,
My mum is everything sweet.

Tom O'Shea
Albermarle Primary School, Wimbledon

Do You Know How I Feel?

I am looking out of my window
I see white policemen with hounds biting the behinds of black people.
You may laugh but trust me, if you were in 1958 and you were black
You would feel the pain as if you were me.

Black people are scared to take a step out of their door.
I would like you to feel my pain, it's like a river of blood,
Well that's how the harassment of the officers makes us feel.

But the saviour, Martin Luther King Jr, is trying to help.
I still see people going against him but no one cares
Us blacks will keep fighting for our rights.
I tell you what it is like,
We can't go to the same hairdressers,
Can't sit in good seats at the cinemas,
Also we have to go to different schools.
Do you know how I feel?

Darius Elliott (10)
Albermarle Primary School, Wimbledon

Feelings

Happiness is the colour blue.
Happiness sounds like children playing,
Happiness feels like the sky,
Happiness tastes like ice cream.

Darkness is the colour black.
Darkness sounds like floorboards creaking,
Darkness feels like rough wood,
Darkness tastes like a horrible sweet.

Love is the colour pink.
Love sounds like peace,
Love feels like a luxurious sofa,
Love tastes like chocolate.

Iman El-Bouzidi (9)
Albermarle Primary School, Wimbledon

Playing Netball

I love playing netball,
I'm glad I am on the team,
When the ball goes in the net
I really want to scream!

I love it when I'm running
And the wind is in my face,
Out on the court
I think I need my space.

I love it with my kit on,
Ready to go,
It is trainers, skirt and shirt,
Not a top hat, waistcoat and bow.

I want to be the captain,
Just to be prepared,
What is the point of netball
If the team is scared?

I love it when I shoot,
Especially when I score,
It feels so great,
I want to score more.

We have to work together,
Bonding as a team,
When we do this
All the people beam.

To score we have to take our time,
What most of us forget,
When we do take our time,
The ball goes in the net.

I love playing netball,
I'm glad I'm on the team.

Ellesse Abbott (9)
Albermarle Primary School, Wimbledon

The Terror Of The War

I suddenly look in the mirror,
I'm twelve years old again.
An evacuee, a victim and an orphan,
Too scared to reveal her name.

Father was off to Germany,
Mother lay in bed.
'Daddy will be home soon,' she said.
Three days later she was dead.

Mother was now dead,
The war is still going.
Dad's now in France,
He's going to have to keep rowing.

Breaking news is in!
Dad was hit by a shell.
Now I have no parents,
Is this the new-found hell?

I now live with a host,
My new home is a farm.
The daughters are polite,
I hope they don't come to harm!

Now I have my children,
In addition, they have children too,
I still pass on stories,
They shall go from me to you.

Sixty-two years have passed,
I had a lot of work to do,
But I can never forget those faithful years,
The years of World War II!

Amy Risley (10)
Albermarle Primary School, Wimbledon

My Mum

In winter my mum is my blanket,
In summer my mum is my shade,
In autumn she is the falling leaf
And in spring she is the smell of the flowers.

Without her my world would be grey
Because she's the colour of my life.

When I get hurt,
My mum suffers the pain.
We're linked in the bond of love
That nobody can break.

The meaning of my life is to keep my mum happy.
She's the one who brought me up and changed my dirty nappy.
She taught me how to talk,
She taught me how to walk.
All the things that I can do are from my lovely mum.

When I am happy my mum is happy,
When I am sad my mum is sad.
When I cry my mum cries.
Everything I do is linked to my mum.

Out of all the relationships there is only one relationship
That you can never have again, and that is your parents.
Once you lose your parents you will never find
Someone else as loving, caring and true as your parents.

Jasmin Chopra (10)
Albermarle Primary School, Wimbledon

My Mum

Roses are red
Violets are blue
I am going to get a baby sister
She might look like you.

I am having another sister
I feel really excited and very happy
But I feel sorry for my one brother
He is the only boy in our house.

Another sister is really nice
The only thing with little girls
You can dress them nicely
And put their hair up and give them good advice.

My mum is very caring
My mum is very loving
My mum is my blanket
And Mummy, I love you.

In the summer my mum is my shade
My mum is a beautiful yellow star
My mum is really cute
And I love her deeply in my heart.

When I love my mum
She always smells like lovely red roses
When the sun shines it gives my mum a smile on her face
Mummy I really, really love you, you are the best mum.

Chloe Adams (9)
Albermarle Primary School, Wimbledon

Although Boxing Is Fun

Although boxing is fun, you still have to run,
To get very fit you will have to skip.
To lose the weight gain you still have to train,
You still have to train and still have to skip
And though boxing is fun, you still have to run.

Although boxing is fun, you still have to run.
Sometimes you get hit if you're too slow to slip.
If you're too slow to slip you'd better be quick.
You still have to train and still have to skip
And still have to slip and need to be quick
And though boxing is fun, you still have to run.

Although boxing is fun, you still have to run,
You must learn to block or you might get a shock.
You need to sidestep or you might hit the deck.
Sometimes you get hit if you're too slow to slip.
If you're too slow to slip you'd better be quick.
You still have to train and still have to skip
And still have to slip and need to be quick
And though boxing is fun, you still have to run.

Rasharn Gabbidon-McLean (9)
Albermarle Primary School, Wimbledon

My London

Some trash, London,
Some bin, London,
Though I'm scared,
Nobody cares.

When I see graffiti
I feel quite sad
Because I know
It's very bad.

Mica Merid (8)
Avonmore Primary School, West Kensington

Living In London

Living in London
Is so smelly cos
People watch telly.
All day long there's pollution
But we've got da solution.

Living in London
Is so cool cos
You can get a mint
Then go for a sprint.

Living in London
Is such fun cos
You can see Big Ben
An' get an egg off a hen.

Living in London
Is so awesome cos
You should go on the London Eye
Then eat a tasty steak pie.

William Taylor (10)
Avonmore Primary School, West Kensington

London Trouble

Ten black cabs standing in Victoria,
Nine children running around with letters,
Eight mums shouting, 'Come here, little devils.'
Seven dads playing snooker in Acton,
Six brothers saying, 'Yo, what's up London?'
Five grans saying, 'Where are my teeth?'
Four horses standing outside Buckingham Palace.
Three red buses standing in Hammersmith.
Two guards eating at Pizza Hut.
One and only *London!*

Savera Khalid (9)
Avonmore Primary School, West Kensington

My Life In London

I wake up on a Monday morning,
I really can't bother,
Talk about unfair, I'm yawning!
So I scream and wake up my mother.

She made me my breakfast,
She said, 'Let me wake up first!'
I said, 'At least I woke up my lazy brother,
The funny things is, I didn't wake up Grandmother!'

I brushed my teeth
And when I spat, out came a leaf!
It must have been all those sweets
I had as a midnight feast.

I went off to school,
In my pocket went my mobile.
I didn't look like a fool,
In fact I dial in style!

I went down the street
Sniffing the air.
Beep, beep, beep,
I wanted to swear
Because of the pollution and noise,
It's a nightmare!

I got to school,
I can't bother, mind you!
Things went through one ear and out the other.
Call me a baby, but I only wanted my mother!

All my friends just gossiped,
I couldn't bother, you know.
All of them had skipped
Some classes, oh!

Well, that's my life in London,
Y'know!

Armaghan Hallajian (10)
Avonmore Primary School, West Kensington

The Best Of London

London is extraordinary
No wonder it's not in the dictionary
There's so much traffic
I really want to panic.

Fish 'n' chips to get da grips
There's Big Ben, lots of gentlemen
There's Tony Blair and Gordon Brown
They always make me frown.

There's a king and queen
They're on the screen
They act all posh
They've got so much dosh.

It's a big city
People are witty
You've got to hold someone's hand
Or you'll get lost in the sand.

The English flag is red and white
It makes a war and puts up a fight.

The music is cool
It's sometimes cruel
So when I'm in my bed
I've got to hold my ted.

Although it's dark
I've got to keep up the march
Or I'll end up like lard.

Georgina Riley (9)
Avonmore Primary School, West Kensington

London

Livin' in London is jus' so cool
Cos
All ov da schools jus' so rule.
Lots ov people luv rock,
Especially people wiv dreadlocks.
Livin' in London is jus' so great,
I don't know 'oo's gonna be me mate.
When I find me mate,
We're gonna stay up late,
We're gonna
Stay in bed,
Rest our head,
Wait until da night is dead.
We're gonna
Play some games,
Call each uvva names.
People at school . . .
Shame!
Endin' da day wiv bangers and mash
Today I've jus' wasted me cash.
I've got enough to buy a ring
An' enough to buy some bling.
Now I can rest me head
In me snug bed.

Eleanor Matthews (9)
Avonmore Primary School, West Kensington

London

B L ack cabs queued up in Paddington
T O wer of London opens and closes
Te N giraffes in London Zoo
Re D phone boxes waiting to be used
P O lice dressed in blue, inspecting,
Big Be N goes ding-dong, ding-dong

The only *London!*

Ammar Roomi (9)
Avonmore Primary School, West Kensington

Da London Rap

Living in da city,
Hard as can be,
But never mind dat,
Everyone is like dat,
So go wid da flow
And no one will ever know.

I ate my breakfast,
I now feel dat I'm in Belfast.
Fish and da chips
Make me move my hips.

Da Central Line is really minging
Like my oyster, it ain't zinging.
Traveling to Hamleys
To see a family.

Living in da city,
Hard as can be,
But never mind dat,
Everyone is like dat,
So go wid da flow
An' no one will ever know, yo!

Elliott Campbell (9)
Avonmore Primary School, West Kensington

London

Ten big buses standing in a row
Nine red phone boxes
Eight stamps on the envelope
Seven buildings in a row
Six people drinking tea
Five big families having a party
Four fish and chips in the pan
Three people having a race
Two trains I can see
And one busy London.

Zahra Hussien (9)
Avonmore Primary School, West Kensington

Fizzy London

London's so cool cos . . .
I wake up in the mornin'
Go to school,
Put on my clothes
'N' brush my teef,
It really, really rules.

All da businessmen goin' to work,
The roads are gettin' busy,
All da traffic beepin', beepin',
London's gettin' all fizzy.

London will give you a smile
Cos technology is getting' higher,
TVs 'n' ringin' mobiles,
Music is on your iPod,
Everything is about style.

All da restaurants,
Fish 'n' chips,
English brekkie,
Move my hips.

London is so sly cos . . .
London is so massive
Wiv Big Ben 'n' London Eye,
All da other places really rock,
Everyone of dem are so high.

And now at da end of da day,
With lunch, supper and sweets,
I say night-night to my mum,
And then I'm fast asleep.

Yllka Fejzullahu (10)
Avonmore Primary School, West Kensington

London

London is cool if you like it,
Which I'm sure you do,
I think I like the London Eye 'n' Big Ben too.
The most common food must be fish 'n' chips,
I think I can give you some tips.
Gangsters can write in graffiti,
Which does look quite cool.

Fergie, Akon 'n' Eminem too,
Sing the best tunes in da house.
London's the best if you think about it,
Cos the Queen does move about.
It is so posh down in London,
You need so much dosh,
To go to da shops cos you can't get enough
Of saying, 'Oh gosh.'

Chloe Hillier (10)
Avonmore Primary School, West Kensington

Living In London

I start the beat with the London heat
And the cars going beat, beat, beat.

As I leap to the fish and chip shop,
There's a cop that tells me to stop.

As I flop to the London Eye,
Oh boy, it's so high!

I'm on da 28 and I'm very, very late
I want to spend my dosh
Cos High Street, Ken' is posh.

I love the trees and the hairy bees
And da birds breed on the trees.

The willow trees show da breeze
An' the sun that makes me *sneeze!*

Jasmine Momeni (10)
Avonmore Primary School, West Kensington

London - London

Every day I see cars,
Big chatty youths out with their pit bulls sniffing,
People out in bars.

London - London.

Hey, but think of the bright side,
There's lots of nice people around my area,
Chatting with me with little strides.

London - London.

I'm going to bed, reading a magazine,
I run downstairs, I call, 'Mum, look.'
I show her a mind-blowing picture of someone
Who can eat a cake in one bite!
It's lunch now, we're having fish and chips,
London is famous for that.

London - London.

That's *my* London and I'm glad,
So you see my London is good
And my London is bad.

Charlotte Evans (8)
Avonmore Primary School, West Kensington

London

Ten big buses standing in a row,
Nine big bridges standing over the river,
Eight fat penguins down in London Zoo,
Seven pink pigs on the city farm,
Six white horses parading at Big Ben,
Five policemen going to a crime,
Four big buildings standing on a street,
Three long tubes down the Underground,
Two big shops standing on Oxford Street,
One big city called London!

Julia Glotova (9)
Avonmore Primary School, West Kensington

London

Trains are noisy in London.
When I go to the airport
People are so noisy
That I could scream my head off.

I see lots of dogs on the streets,
Going bark, bark on the streets of London.
The dogs stink so bad I could go back home
And start crying in London.

We won the cup in the children's
Football match in London on Thursday.
London is so fat,
It looks like a giant elephant.

If London was a person,
It would sound like this,
The person would be fat because
There are lots of people in London.

The colour of the person would be grey
Because the ground is grey.
The best part about London is
Lots of family are together.
I care about my family more than anything,
More than London.

Onyinyechi Okorie (8)
Avonmore Primary School, West Kensington

London

In London it is very busy
And in London I always get dizzy.
In London I hear cars on the road,
In London I normally hear loads.
In London I hear on the news gun crime
And hear children whine.
In London there are loads of people,
I couldn't count them all, but most of them are tall!

Ned Prevezer (8)
Avonmore Primary School, West Kensington

London

I don't like London
Because they abandon,
But I've got a good teacher
Called Mr Crandon.
London is busy,
That's what I like
But the thing is,
London has gangsters.
I don't like gangsters
Because they make
London messy,
By putting
Graffiti all
Over the place.
When I go to school
And I have a school race,
I sometimes win
Because I always have the pace.
But I'm not very happy
Because the gangsters are
Not doing their education,
The gangsters go to vacation.
I don't like living here,
I sometimes fear.

Darnell Tetteh (8)
Avonmore Primary School, West Kensington

The Big And Gigantic

There are dogs and cars all round
and I am thankful and am happy for school and friends
and a teacher who is very funny
and also a very cross man
In London there are lots of animals and a lot of people.

Thubelihle Mguni (8)
Avonmore Primary School, West Kensington

My London

London is my cold but lovely home,
It is OK, but I'd rather live somewhere
Greener and have more nature.
I hear very strange noises.

There are too many noisy, polluting cars,
Loads of parks, so many houses
And I do not like London.

There are so many drunk people
And shouting people,
I also feel happy in London,
People are so friendly.

I feel welcome when I come back to London,
It's like a big man.
London City is not all good,
I do not like the gangsters and graffiti,
And the gangsters show off.

Alice Center (8)
Avonmore Primary School, West Kensington

London

There is po   L   lution in the air,
It is very bad, y   O   u can't not care.
Every day you ca   N   hear the cars,
And all the chil   D   ren like chocolate bars.
Me living in L   O   ndon is pretty boring,
Unless you hear a   N   aeroplane soaring,

You can hear the   B   ig Ben making a noise,
And you can hea   R   the noise of the girls and boys,
There are the tax   I   cabs taking people away,
There are also   D   ogs all through the day.
The London Eye   G   oes round and round,
And now w   E   must not make a sound.

Eve Staheli (9)
Avonmore Primary School, West Kensington

My London

London is noisy,
Parks are famous for me.
There's many markets.
London is my mate,
I go to school in London.
There are not many holidays to go to.
London is sweet,
There's lots of perfumes.
London is dusty,
Dust is on the floor.
My mum shuts the door
While I clean the floor.
I eat more desserts
While my mum goes swimming.
I rush to the park,
My brother starts to cry,
I say, 'Shush, shush, I'll die.'

Noor Zaini (8)
Avonmore Primary School, West Kensington

One Beautiful City

Ten red buses lining up at Earl's Court
Nine people waving to the Queen
Eight horses walking on the road
Seven black cabs in High Street, Kensington
Six trains in Olympia
Five policemen walking on the street
Four double-decker buses going to Kew Gardens
Three men fixing Big Ben
Two limos next to Hyde Park
One beautiful city.

Jennifer Bazilyuk (9)
Avonmore Primary School, West Kensington

Great Old London

It's fantastic,
It's fun,
It's safe,
Don't be scared,
Just come to it,
Come on it.
Tiny to me,
But giant to you,
It's cool,
It's good,
Come, it's time
To come here,
Today's the day,
Come on now,
Come over,
Have some fun.
London, he's the man,
He's got rubbish
All over him
But he's got
Pockets full
Of gold,
Silver, copper.
He's got
People walking
All over him,
But he doesn't care,
He's cool,
He's great,
But most of all,
He's fun.

Finlay Watson (7)
Avonmore Primary School, West Kensington

What Should I Do?

What should I do today?
What should I do today?
What should I do today?
What should I do?
Should I go to Piccadilly,
Or stay at home with little Billy?
Should I go to London Bridge,
Or go to eat some fish and chips?
Should I take the warm, dry train,
Or just go through the pouring rain?
What should I do today?
What should I do today?
What should I do today?
What should I do?
It's just a typical London day,
So what should I do today?

Dhuha Sajjad (9)
Avonmore Primary School, West Kensington

In London

In London . . .

Ten horses parading at Buckingham Palace
Nine tubes queuing in a cube
Eight police guarding The Houses of Parliament
Seven black cabs driving down the lane
Six people visiting the Canary Wharf
Five seconds till New Year's Day countdown in Oxford Street
Four sightseeing buses at Westminster Abbey
Three people praying at St Paul's
Two red buses in Hyde Park
And one busy London.

Saffa Abdi (8)
Avonmore Primary School, West Kensington

London

Twenty people being frightened at the London Dungeon,
Nineteen deer at Richmond Park,
Eighteen police on bicycles,
Seventeen wax models at Madame Tussaud's,
Sixteen boats racing on the River Thames,
Fifteen black cabs with people waiting,
Fourteen shiny red postboxes,
Thirteen stamps waiting to be used,
Twelve cars waiting to cross Tower Bridge,
Eleven train carriages to Brighton,
Ten sightseeing buses being driven around London,
Nine fish 'n' chips on the bench,
Eight people working in the Gherkin,
Seven shops being opened in Oxford Street,
Six bags being held by Kate Moss,
Five busy junctions all with traffic jams,
Four horses parading at Buckingham Palace,
Three people on the London Eye,
Two museums all about history,
One London! (In Britain)

Alice Armstrong (9)
Avonmore Primary School, West Kensington

Animals

In London there are ten dogs that are playing on a log
And there are nine mice that are playing on a log.
There are eight birds sitting on a plate
And there are seven wasps biting a block.
There are six horses running in first place.
There are five jumping on boots.
There are four monkeys biting their knees.
There are three bears walking down the stairs.
There are two fishes swimming in the sea.
There is one cat running to its pet bee.

Omar Harb (9)
Avonmore Primary School, West Kensington

Livin' In London

Livin' in London is really cool,
It really rules,
Lookin' out of da window
I see Big Ben tickin' da town,
Oh no da sun is goin' down.

Da next day I head for fish 'n' chips,
Yum, yum, yum, now for some drinks.
Let's go to da London Eye,
Boy it's so high,
Up and up there's da Queen
Sittin' on her chair gettin' her servants to comb her hair.

Da London Bridge is where I hang out,
'N' where my friends are about.
From there we head to Kings Mall
To see all da bangin' shops,
To buy some tops and sweet lollipops.

As I walk home my feet ache,
Now I got a headache.
I pause 'n' stare at da river,
It's making me shiver.
Finally I'm home,
Now I can rest,
Even though my sister is a pest.

Aya Saleh (9)
Avonmore Primary School, West Kensington

London War

London is a very bad place
Because there are bad people
Killing with guns and knives
And are robbing the city

London is like a dog
Because there are bricks.

Samuel Apaijitt (7)
Avonmore Primary School, West Kensington

Living In London

Transport is so mingin'
Bikes well they're jus' ringin'
Buying all da chips I can eat
Goin' with da London beat
I'm on da London Eye
An' I jus' see dat I can fly
Seein' all da scenery
London's got a lot of greenery
Did ya know dat London's so cool?
They're by far the best at football

Buyin' all da things I see
Hope I'm in time for tea

Buy a pack of bubblegum
Maybe jus' a little plum
Walking back home again
London can be quite a pain
Jus' lyin' on da settee
Maybe watch some telly
'Night, night Ted'
I'm goin' to bed.

Duff Westmoreland (10)
Avonmore Primary School, West Kensington

Life In London

In London ten red buses lined up in a queue
In London nine fish and chips were cooking for dinner
In London eight black cabs collecting people
In London seven policemen working in Oxford Street
In London six trains going to the London Zoo
In London five people waving to the Queen
In London four red post boxes standing in a row
In London three clowns in Piccadilly Circus
In London two people swimming on a boat in the River Thames
In London one Big Ben in the centre of London.

Kate Bazilyuk (9)
Avonmore Primary School, West Kensington

My London Rap

The traffic is so noisy
you can't hear yourself fink.

The scenery is so 'bui'ful
includin' the Queen's bling.
I lost my bling so I stole
da Queen's ring.

Da police sirens ran after
me to da end of London.
I paid them 800 pounds
and they let me go
so I went to the globe.

Shakespeare wrote a play
with a zing about mi 'n' my 'folks'.

Money is like a disease
people get so selfish.

At the end I go home
I get the remo
I turn on the TV and watch CBBC.

Maya Harnady (10)
Avonmore Primary School, West Kensington

Tube Where Are You Going?

Where's the Tube?
It's in Hyde Park
It's in Stamford Brook
It's at the Science Museum
It's at Buckingham Palace
Where's the Tube?
It's at the fish and chip shop
It's near the red buses
It's at the Tower of London
It's at the London Eye
It's nowhere, just here.

Andy Tarshalla (9)
Avonmore Primary School, West Kensington

Livin' In Da City London

London is so really cool
As we walk away from school
When we sit in da parks
I think and hope I get good marks
Even though school doesn't rule
In fact it kind of even drools.

Livin' in flat is so nice
Sittin' on da table eatin' rice
I must not eat any sweeties
Especially since I have diabetes.

The London buses just drive
But they're good when you need to see somfin live
At the gigs the baldies wear wigs
As the dogs doo doo and dig.

London is so really cool
As we walk away from school
After goin' on da London Eye
There's lots of souvenirs to buy
When I look at Big Ben it tick-tocks
And turns 10am so then I go and eat my snack
Two minutes later I'll be back.

Playin' tennis against a boy called Dennis
Yeah he is a menace
Never mind like I won
Now I think my work here is done.

Phoebe Watts (10)
Avonmore Primary School, West Kensington

My Life

Rich people,
Poor people everywhere,
I know it's my home right here.
I go to school,
Go home
And to the park.
I hear music everywhere,
Pop and rock.

I feel sad,
I feel glad,
Happy and all those things.
I try to sit and relax,
Then my doorbell rings.
It's a rich man,
It's a poor man,
It's a holy preacher.
They want to talk to my parents.
It's my teacher.

So this is . . .
My life!

Olivia Traverso Madden (9)
Avonmore Primary School, West Kensington

London

Ten big black cabs in a queue
Nine tubes in a hurry at Paddington Station
Eight innocent people locked up at London Dungeons
Seven police having fish and chips
Six sightseeing buses full of tourists
Five fishermen fishing at the River Thames
Four people posting letters through the red post boxes
Three guards surrounding Buckingham Palace
Two of each animal in a cage in London Zoo
One London we live in.

Marwa Abdi (8)
Avonmore Primary School, West Kensington

Friendship

F unny
R eliable
I maginative
E xcellent
N aughty
D aring
S weet
H appy
I nteresting
P layful.

Rachael Kingsley (10)
Eardley Primary School, Streatham

The Master

As the sun sets on a snowy scene,
A mysterious track can be found
Belonging to a silver shadow
With bushy tail and slender leg,
A haunting howl and superb skill.
Timber wolf. Master wolf.

Hebe Perry-Belfrage (10)
Eardley Primary School, Streatham

Wonders Of The Sun - Tanka

Going down at night,
Invincible you are not,
We rely on you,
You are so immaculate,
Why are you a dying star?

Berthram Silvera (11)
Eardley Primary School, Streatham

If

If you stand in the sun
You will burn like a bun.
If you don't recycle,
You're the Devil's disciple.
If you cut the rainforest trees,
The animals won't be pleased.
If the environment is a failure,
Then you'll need more than an inhaler.
If you don't want to use your motorbike,
Then go for a hike.
If you don't save water,
The earth may be slaughtered.
If you drive,
You may not be alive.
If you walk,
You still may be able to talk.

Tierney Glide (11)
Eardley Primary School, Streatham

The Red Irania

The Red Irania floated on the water,
She slid smoothly on the water
While the waves splashed gently on her side.
Crish, crash.
The wind blew her across the flowing water,
The water rippled.
The setting sun went down in the far distance.
A gust of wind blew The Red Irania onto some rocks,
Water filled the boat.
The Red Irania was sinking.

Fanxi Liu (8)
Eardley Primary School, Streatham

School Rules

One at a time,
Keep in the line
Or I will give you a fine.
Don't talk, walk!
Have fun
But don't run,
Don't bully,
Respect fully . . .

Sit on the floor,
Close the door,
Don't play on the stairs,
Get in pairs,
Stop making that silly noise.
Do me a favour, girls and boys
Make lots of noise!

Tamicha Rochester-Prosper (10)
Eardley Primary School, Streatham

Pollution Poem

Pollution is all around us,
It's all in the air,
Young children are dying
But nobody cares.

It's killing and hurting people,
All caused by cars.
Don't drive when you can walk,
Save the environment and start to walk far.

This could be our only hope,
So help us and walk,
Or will the world be no more?

Zandria Vas (10)
Eardley Primary School, Streatham

If

If you don't climb trees you won't hurt your knees
If you pay attention you won't be in detention
If the environment needs saving you better start behaving
If you get out the car your health will go far
If you walk to school, you'll keep the planet cool
If you get on your bike you can go on a hike
If you open your eyes you can see the sunrise
If you help the Earth stay cool you won't be a fool
If you don't change your ways it will shorten your days.

Marisa, Janna & Daniele (11)
Eardley Primary School, Streatham

Love

Love is cherry red,
It tastes like ripe red apples
And it smells like lovely strawberries.
It looks like soapy bubbles floating in the air.
Love makes me feel like there are thousands of
                            butterflies in my belly.

Nneka Williams (10)
Eardley Primary School, Streatham

If

If you drive your car
The world will turn black.
If we don't find a solution for this
We will not have a resolution for this confusion.
If we don't drive cars,
We won't be behind bars.

Esosa Uwaifo (11)
Eardley Primary School, Streatham

The Dangerous Volcanoes

Hot, dangerous volcanoes,
Lava pops out as people shout,
It erupts fast like lightning, then it becomes frightening.
The Earth's crust finds its way through
So it can explode as big as a mountain.
It turns into rocks after the explosion,
You hear it go *boom, bang,*
And you have to leave as quickly as you can.

Corey Nurse (10)
Eardley Primary School, Streatham

Don't Drive

You drive to drop off your kids,
But you don't care about the traffic.
You waste money on petrol only to pollute the air.
Walk to save money, if only you cared,
But if you couldn't drive
It would be worthwhile,
So walk for exercise to get fit.

Hassan Mahmud (11)
Eardley Primary School, Streatham

Love

Love is an electric-red,
Love tastes like strawberries,
Love smells like freshly picked roses,
Love looks like hearts,
Love sounds like a wedding,
Love feels like the warmth of someone's heart.

Luke Lacriarde (10)
Eardley Primary School, Streatham

Tops Pizza

Toppings pizza,
It's my favourite,
I wish I went there today.

Pizza, pizza,
Toppings pizza,
It's a fun delight.

Pizza, pizza,
Toppings pizza,
It's, I know, the Queen's favourite dish.

Pizza, pizza,
Toppings pizza,
It's pineapple and fish.

I have pizza, pizza time
At Tops pizza.

Fatima Sunni (9)
Eardley Primary School, Streatham

If

If you look after the environment,
It will look after you.
If you don't stop the pollution
There will be more floods
And that's the solution.
If we drive our cars all day
We will surely burn away.
If you walk to school,
There will be less asthma, you fool!
If you recycle more paper,
There will be more trees.

Mohamed Aden (11)
Eardley Primary School, Streatham

Violence And Bullets!

Let's stop the violence in our world!
Let's help people less fortunate than us,
Let it be safe to get on the bus,
Let's not be scared to big ourselves up.

So come on,
Let's go outside,
Don't be afraid,
There's no need to hide.

People are terrified to leave their houses
Because of the wannabe gangsters
And their loud mouths.
Bang! Another life is gone, lying on the street.

That is why everyone says
Let's live life to its fullest,
Let's start fresh,
Without any violence or bullets!

Jhelisa Graham (11)
Eardley Primary School, Streatham

Save The World

We need to save this phenomenal Earth,
Because if we don't it will never rebirth,
And this Earth was not man-made,
So if we don't act soon, the world will fade.
We can stop polluting the air,
Because we might soon be in despair.
The glaciers are melting at an alarming rate,
We have got to stop this because we may soon be at our fate.
We have already witnessed this terrible warming
And I hope, my friends, this gives you a warning.
50 billion tonnes of ice have gone in less than a month.
We need to *save the world!*

Sebastian Sandhir (10)
Eardley Primary School, Streatham

Sports

Taking part
Fitness
Competitive
Charged up
Obsessed
So good
Explosive
Excitement
Overwhelming.
This is what sport gives to me.

Losing
Still gives joy
I've tried
A lesson
Disappointment
Numb
Speechless
Frustration
Understanding
Know myself
Extraordinary
Everyone loses sometimes.

Victory
Makes you reap the rewards again and again
Very exciting
Makes you want to jump around
It makes you want to win again
This is what victory is about
It could happen to you one day.

Terentino Mills & Kofi Amaadzie (10)
Eardley Primary School, Streatham

The View!

The view from my window
Is not that amazing,
But still here I sit,
Wondering and gazing.

Alone in my room,
Watching the planes go by,
Watching and watching
Until they fade in the sky.

The view from my car
Is different all the way,
It changes and changes,
Like March, April and May.

Sitting in the back of my car,
Looking through the window,
Someone is watching me,
Is she a friend or foe?

The view form the plane
Is blue and white,
Looking through the window
And nothing else is in sight.

Calling the flight attendant
To ask for a drink,
Gazing out the window
As I start to think

What a beautiful view!

Sabrina Rafiq (11)
Eardley Primary School, Streatham

Teachers - Haiku

Coffee-smelling breath
Bad-tempered, shout deafeningly
Lazy but noisy.

Akhirah Hulcome (11)
Eardley Primary School, Streatham

Hate

Hate is when a bundle of emotions comes tight and makes
                                        the world suffer.
Hate is a cruel and evil word saying, 'I wish you were dead.'
Hate is when you become heartless and you don't know
                                        when it will end.
Hate can be envy or sadness,
Let's hope it doesn't creep up on you.

Tyler Moore (11)
Eardley Primary School, Streatham

Pollution

Pollution is destroying us and yet we still use cars and buses.
If we don't stop causing pollution, we'll be something of the past.
Can we walk on the Earth without harming it?
I wonder if anyone can have fun because of
The pollution destroying everything in its path.
Stop using cars, buses, vans and trucks and walk,
Because it may be our only chance.

Yonis Nur (11)
Eardley Primary School, Streatham

Vicious Speed

V icious speed
O ccupied to kill
L ifeless
C ool, hot lava
A ngry lava
N othing can stop it
O ccupied to let out grey gas
E rupted
S till standing . . .

Teeyana Graham (10)
Eardley Primary School, Streatham

Alone

No one is alone,
Even if you think
No one is your friend,
You are wrong.

In the world, many people live,
You don't know if they like you
Or if they don't.

I know that everyone has a friend
And I know because I'm everyone's friend
And always shall be.

Maya Sharda (8)
Eardley Primary School, Streatham

Anger!

It's as dark as a winter's night,
A shiver to the spine.
Blood boils, like a cauldron bubbling and brewing,
Until it erupts like a volcano,
Shooting off in every direction.
Anger smells putrid,
Anger is here,
Anger is in the air.

Aaron Matteus-Hendricks (11)
Eardley Primary School, Streatham

Walk

W alk to school, stops pollution
A ll kinds of pollution are dangerous
L ove the planet, do not torture the planet
K eep safe and care for the planet.

Layla Dhiman (8)
Eardley Primary School, Streatham

Walk To School

W alk, never drive
A lways stay away from the car
L ook when you cross the road
K eep healthy

T ake pollution away
O pen the door and walk to school

S tay safe
C ars make pollution
H elp stop pollution
O nly walk
O xygen dies
L ook out.

Quinn Mireku (8)
Eardley Primary School, Streatham

Walk To School

W alk, don't drive
A lways walk
L et's walk to school
K eep healthy

T he kids get energy
O nly walk, don't run

S tay safe
C hildren in the park
H ey, come on and stop pollution
O pen your eyes, look
O pen your door and smell all the fresh air
L ook out.

Zaiba Nadeem (8)
Eardley Primary School, Streatham

The Frog

Frogs are blobs,
Frogs are weird,
Frogs have no ears,
Frogs have big eyes
That stick out of their heads.

Roses are red,
Frogs are green,
Some people think
This is obscene.

Lily Dovey-Linke (8)
Eardley Primary School, Streatham

Baseball

Baseball is fun
Until you make a home run,
You wish it was done.
The ball you swing goes too far
Then ends up hitting a baseball car.
A player can't hear
Because the audience always cheer.
The blue team jump in the air
And they don't play fair.

Ephraim Conteh (8)
Eardley Primary School, Streatham

Excitement

Excitement is glittery,
Excitement tastes like strawberries,
It smells like ripe bananas
And looks like loads of presents.
It sounds like laughter and happiness
And feels like flowers in my hair.

Sakina Kashmiri (10)
Eardley Primary School, Streatham

My Name Is Angel

I have tears like stars falling from the dark, dim sky.
My name is Angel.
I glide through the dusty clouds
While my wings are gleaming,
Leaving shadows down below.
My name is Angel.
I have hands that glitter,
That comfort sad faces.
My name is Angel.
I have smiles that never
Turn upside down.
My name is Angel
And I am glad to be one.

Samirah Oyede (9)
Eardley Primary School, Streatham

A Gun

A gun is a soldier's friend
A gun is a soldier's saviour
A gun brings people to Heaven
A gun sends people to Hell
A gun is wicked
As evil as a devil
A gun is brilliant
In fact, fabulous
A gun travels from country to country
A gun travels from sea to land
No one knows
Bloody killer
Or saviour.

David Wan (11)
Eardley Primary School, Streatham

Walk To School

W rap up warm if it's cold
A cat walking by
L ook left and right
K eep aware of the traffic

T ogether we can save the world
O pen your eyes

S top pollution before it's too late
C rows flying by up in the sky
H appy days without pollution
O ver the hills
O ver the logs
L ook towards the sunlight.

Clare Stringer (8)
Eardley Primary School, Streatham

Life And Trust

Life is a thing that you feel in your heart, in your soul,
It's not about being silly or being rude,
It's about enjoying yourself,
Helping each other,
Loving your family,
Supporting each other.

Trust is about believing in yourself,
Believing in each other.
Trust is about telling the truth.

Renee Guisle (9)
Eardley Primary School, Streatham

Invasion

Bloodthirsty aliens, we're under attack,
We can't hold them back for long.
The army have done all they can,
They have breached all of our strongholds.
We can't survive for long,
We have a limited amount of food and water.
Ammo levels are dropping,
The ground is shaking,
The stench is growing.
They're getting nearer,
There seems to be no way out.
Nothing more we can do.
Oh no, they're here!

Jazzim Saroochi (10)
Eardley Primary School, Streatham

If Disaster Strikes

Global warming is making disaster,
We need a master,
A master of every element,
Who can stop smog and fog.
If God is our only hope,
Also God's not to blame,
Rather, He is our Father.
If only we had responsibility,
We shouldn't burn items,
We shouldn't waste paper,
We shouldn't ever cause pollution,
If only we had respect for our world.

Fahd Arif (12)
Eardley Primary School, Streatham

Create A Safe Place!

Melting, melting,
Wasting away,
So I say,
Create a place,
Create a safe place.

Scientists are amazed
At the speed of the fall
Of the great ice wall,
Create a place,
Create a safe place.

Please help the environment,
Half of the problems are from our homes,
Especially mobile phones,
Create a place,
Create a safe place.

The ice is melting,
Too much damage is being done,
All because of the burning sun,
Create a place,
Create a safe place.

Ella Rimmer (10)
Eardley Primary School, Streatham

Martial Arts

My dream
A martial artist
High kicks
Strong punches
All the pain from stretching
I will succeed
Motivation from Dad
'It will be useful'
Thinking ahead
My future.

Khalil Lafta (11)
Eardley Primary School, Streatham

I Am A Little Girl

I am a little girl, small in sight,
Deep inside me there is love,
I have discovered that I live in the light.
You shouldn't judge a person,
Is that right?
I spend time thinking,
How can I make things better?
That is the reason why
I'm so bright!

Charesia Patten (11)
Eardley Primary School, Streatham

Global Warming

Global warming is tearing us apart.
Global warming is breaking our hearts.
Global warming is burning our souls.
Global warming is heating us like coal.
Global warming is causing us to die.
Global warming is warming the sky.
Global warming is destroying our future.
Global warming is killing our nature.

Yuyi Kabanje & Romello Armani-Cozier (11)
Eardley Primary School, Streatham

Dad!

Loving man
Caring person
Taxi driver
Trip taker
Always there for you
Never doubt about him.

Lareb Naseem (11)
Eardley Primary School, Streatham

Global Warming

Global warming is changing and forming
In the world that is storming.
Children are very scared,
But how would people stop global warming?
It's trying to tell us that's a warning,
Global warming is causing different things
But it gives people all sorts of tinkles.
People would really care.
If global warming sets a disaster,
We will really need a master.
Global warming is killing the world,
Then we will end up like a huge twirl.

Rebecca Thompson (11)
Eardley Primary School, Streatham

What We Do

The world seems to be coming to an end
Because we have not been the environment's best friend.
We drive our cars around,
We see the clouds beginning to frown.
Rubbish is dumped on our streets,
Green grass is paved with concrete.
We should appreciate our environment
By watching what we do,
Carefully recycling our rubbish,
Both me and you.

Jade Mitchell (8)
Eardley Primary School, Streatham

Life

To look at life
Is to look at an adventure.
Exploring and learning,
Whatever the weather,
Having fun day by day,
Together.

Everything around us
Is a beautiful sight,
Growing in beauty
Night after night.
Ungrateful as we are,
We still get to live without a fight.

This world, for us,
In our lives we must treasure.
Look after it,
Reward it forever and ever.
Sadly it's being destroyed
And it's changing our weather.

Again, to look at life,
Is to look at an adventure.
So we must use our lives
And save where we live together.
Make it a fantastic experience,
A journey, an adventure.

Chinyere Logan (11)
Eardley Primary School, Streatham

Anger

Anger feels like a volcano erupting,
Anger smells like burning fire,
Anger looks like a dustbin,
Anger sounds like a door slamming,
Anger tastes like worms.

William Duncan Dennis-Hoare (10)
Eardley Primary School, Streatham

Volcano

Volcanoes glow
And it's not so slow.
Volcanoes spark
With lots of bark
With tiny stones
And great giant bones.
People shout
While the magma comes out.
Babies are crying
While the trees are dying.
People are running
Furthermore the lava is
Very stunning.
The lava has gone crazy
And the man across the
Road is very lazy.
So everyone run
And it won't be fun
That is to say
So go far away
And here's my advice
Don't come back.

Pooja Vara (10)
Eardley Primary School, Streatham

'If' Pollution

Global warming will cause drought if we don't act now,
Pollution is toxic and will cause doom all around.
If you knew what would happen, you would be stunned.
The amount of evil, ferocious and heart-killing pollutants
Would swallow your head away.
If we don't act now, the pollution will overcome
The spinning sphere we call Earth!

Danial Khan (10)
Eardley Primary School, Streatham

The Endless Love

Love sounds like violins playing slow, romantic music
With gushes of love flowing through the sky.
It looks like a pink and orange sunset with a yellow sun.
It smells like a sweet-scented perfume.
It tastes like caramel chocolate with fudge in the middle.
Its colour is flames of red and pink hearts everywhere.
It feels like there's an arm here and there,
You feel warm and cuddly.
Love reminds me of when I'm in bed all snugly.

Ruka Yussuff (10)
Loughborough Primary School, Brixton

Love!

Love is red like a beautiful rose.
Love tastes like a scrumptious candy cane dipped in honey.
Love feels like red silk on your bed sheets.
Love smells like a handful of petals.
Love reminds me of chocolates in a heart-shaped box.
Love sounds like a rainfall in the jungle.

Loretta Yussuff
Loughborough Primary School, Brixton

Love

Love is happiness like you love someone.
Love is red like a top which you're wearing.
It sounds like butterflies,
It tastes like sweets which you see in your garden like flowers.
Love looks like a heart that you have.
Love feels like you're in bed sleeping tight.

Veneisha Seymour (10)
Loughborough Primary School, Brixton

A Beautiful Island

A beautiful island just for me,
Green grass slithering like snakes,
Stars beaming as hard as fire,
The cold breeze whistling along,
The beautiful blue sky just like the sea,
The beautiful island is all for me,
The moon is like a big fireball,
Trees waving from side to side
Looking like people waving their hands.
The beautiful island is all for me.

Ridwan Jamir (8)
Loughborough Primary School, Brixton

Happiness

Happiness is colourful like a beautiful, wonderful rainbow.
Happiness sounds like two lovely couples being married.
Happiness tastes like sweet and delicate strawberries.
Happiness smells like delicious, juicy mango.
Happiness looks like two best friends laughing.
Happiness feels like a dream come true.
Happiness reminds me of a long, kind holiday.

Siobhan Charles (8)
Loughborough Primary School, Brixton

Anger

Anger is red like someone jumping in the fire,
It feels like you are red,
It smells like aliens destroying the Earth,
It looks like the sun burning the world,
It reminds me of being angry.
It sounds like alien noises coming to Earth,
It tastes like hot food burning in your mouth.

Abdi Mohamed (9)
Loughborough Primary School, Brixton

Love

Love is red like a delicious sweet strawberry falling from the
most beautiful sky.
Love reminds me of my mum and dad hugging.
Love smells like the most wonderful rose.
Love looks like two couples getting married.
Love sounds like someone singing a song.
Love feels like a smooth pillow.
Love tastes like raspberry ice cream.

Esther Olowu (9)
Loughborough Primary School, Brixton

Happiness

Happiness is colourful like a long colourful rainbow.
Happiness sounds like beautiful people getting married.
Happiness tastes like red, delicious, incredible strawberries.
Happiness smells like sweet-smelling roses.
Happiness reminds me of my family having fun.
Happiness looks like shiny, colourful lights.

Shanieke Scott (8)
Loughborough Primary School, Brixton

Fear

Fear is black like the night sky,
It smells like burning wood in the dark forest.
It tastes like a crumbling volcano,
It feels like a hot, blazing fire,
It reminds me of before the world began.
It sounds like people eating and crashing ice.
It looks like a black hairy spider.

Evelyn-Chipo-Mariott-Makuka (9)
Loughborough Primary School, Brixton

Anger

Anger is red like lava exploding out of a volcano!
Anger is fearless like the Devil stuck in Hell trying to
                              defeat the great God.
Anger feels like you're getting burnt by soup.
Anger sounds like the world's worst earthquake.
Anger tastes like five chillies in your mouth.
Anger looks like a building burning down in flames.
Anger smells like a chicken that is burnt.

Ashley McGibbon (9)
Loughborough Primary School, Brixton

Anger

Anger is the colour of purple.
Anger sounds like a fierce dragon.
Anger tastes like gooey cheese.
Anger smells like expired food.
Anger feels like the sun is going to burn your skin.
Anger looks like you're going to burst into millions of pieces.
Anger reminds me of drowning in the sea.

Sherifah Abdul (8)
Loughborough Primary School, Brixton

Anger

Anger is red like fire.
Anger smells like bitterness.
Anger tastes like feet.
Anger sounds like danger.
Anger feels like a tornado.
Anger looks like mayhem.
Anger reminds me of my mum.

Emmanuel Smith (8)
Loughborough Primary School, Brixton

Across The Horizon

Come outside,
The grass is moving like trees swaying,
The moon is shining like a light,
The light is shining like a witch moving her wand,
The heart of the land.

Come outside,
They are having a good time,
The dogs are barking like thunder,
The heart of the land.

Come outside,
The wind is as fast as a car,
A car is like the wind,
Love in the air like fairies,
Houses lighting up like candles,
Stars shining like the sun,
Dragonflies like houses glimmering,
The heart of the land.

Leon McClancy (7)
Loughborough Primary School, Brixton

Across The Horizon

Come across the garden,
See the moon as bright as stars,
Light shining bright in houses,
Yellow T-shirts glowing in the dark,
Noisy dogs barking aloud,
Heart land.

Come across the garden,
See the trees waving like hands in the air,
Hear the singing like sweet swan chocolate,
Grass as green as a snake sliding down a hill,
Heart land.

Tyler Fraser
Loughborough Primary School, Brixton

Sun Setting

Stars shining as bright as the moon,
The moon as round as the sun,
Stars as high as the earth below,
Moon up high to watch us!
Heart of Tobago.

Sun setting,
Houses as bright as the sun,
Peaceful music playing,
Bright lights flashing one by one,
Love spreading all around,
Heart of Tobago.

Sun shining,
Nature all around,
Fireflies flying sporadically,
Birds falling asleep like daffodils,
Chipmunks crawling to their nests,
Heart of Tobago.

Chloe McGovern (7)
Loughborough Primary School, Brixton

I Love You

Her love is like a blanket that holds me tight,
Which keeps me safe and warm all throughout the night.
I love her very much, from the bottom of my heart,
She is always around and I hope we never part.
She is always there for me,
She taught me how to care,
We share a bond so sacred that nothing can compare.
I love this woman so,
To me there is no other,
This special person in my life
Is my dear and loving mother.

Zhané Smith (10)
Loughborough Primary School, Brixton

Archie, My Mad Dog

I have a dog,
His name is Archie,
He annoys my dad
'Cause he chews on his slipper.

He thinks it's
His Sunday dinner.
Archie licks his tummy,
I think it's very funny.

Archie runs on the lawn
Like he's just been born.
He chases birds,
Like he's very mad.

But it doesn't matter
'Cause the birds are too fast.

Olayiwola Amire (10)
Loughborough Primary School, Brixton

My Poem

Fear is black like the night sky,
It sounds like an exploding volcano,
It tastes like a boiling sausage,
It reminds me of the boiling hot sun.

Love is pink like a hot rose lying in the sun.
It looks like a beautiful horizon so far.
Love smells like a fragrant rose.

Happiness is yellow like the brilliant glimmering sun.
Happiness sounds like dolphins squeaking.
Happiness looks like a cute animal.

Ben Breach (10)
Loughborough Primary School, Brixton

If Tears
(In memory of my mum who died of cancer two years ago)

If tears could build a stairway and memory a lane,
I would walk right up to Heaven and bring my mum back down again.

I miss her so much it hurts inside sometimes
I feel so weak sometimes I have to sit down
If I only had one wish, that would be to see my mum again
My heart keeps beating but there is no healing
I picture her face, her smile, her loving way
I keep dreaming of seeing her one day.

If tears could build a stairway and memory a lane
I would walk right up to Heaven and bring my mum back down again.

Britney Piggott (11)
Loughborough Primary School, Brixton

Cutty Sark

Cutty Sark, Cutty Sark,
Went on fire near Greenwich Park.
Fire blazed everywhere,
People shouted, 'Look over there!'

It was made in 1869,
People thought the ship would be fine.
All of a sudden, came some flames,
Everyone thought it was just a shame.

Cutty Sark
Burned in the dark,
No more tea
From across the China Sea.

The ship burned,
The figurehead was fine,
All that was earned
Is now on the line.

Andrew Breach (11)
Loughborough Primary School, Brixton

Love

Love feels like a beautiful rose hanging from a tree.
Love feels like a wonderful fragrance just sitting beside you.
Love feels like a rose bursting from the sky but all you can see is
Petals falling like a beautiful, warm, cuddly raindrop.
Love smells like an adorable, beautiful bush filled
With the most amazing roses in all towns.
Love tastes like a sugary chocolate cake
But all you can see are the most amazing roses ever.
Love tastes like melting, delicious, scrumptious strawberry bars
With the most adorable roses and with the most
Scrumptious pudding, chocolate cake and custard cream.
Love smells like the most amazing rose.

Nataskie Wright (9)
Loughborough Primary School, Brixton

Around Me
*(This poem is dedicated to all my wonderful teachers
who helped me to get this far)*

Behind me
Is Loughborough School,
Little kids waving goodbye.

Above me
At Loughborough School
Ceiling light asking me why.

Around me
At Loughborough School
See me and my mates bawling our eyes out.

Beside me
At Loughborough School
All these hands encouraging me
About my new school
Around me.

Sawida Bedor-Bangura (10)
Loughborough Primary School, Brixton

Fear Poem

Fear sound like a big wave coming out of the volcano,
It tastes like a burning flame, as if someone put a matchstick
                              to my mouth and burned it.
It smells like grey smoke curling around your nose.
It feels like you're gonna faint.
Fear looks like a fierce lion roaring.
It feels like pins stabbing into your heart.
It reminds me of a steaming vegetable about to burst.

Sergen Etam (10)
Loughborough Primary School, Brixton

Feelings

Love is pink like Cupid's heart.
Love is pink like a beautiful, fragrant rose.
It sounds like your heart is about to explode.
Love tastes like a box of delicious chocolates.
It smells like our beautiful fresh air.
It looks like doves flying around in the air.

Reece Gayle (10)
Loughborough Primary School, Brixton

Loneliness

Loneliness is like a broken heart.
Loneliness is an orphan trying to find its mother and father.
It's like a lost person waiting to be picked up.
Loneliness is a lost, sad feeling.
No one loves you.

Jahmarley Gibson
Loughborough Primary School, Brixton

Fly Away

Fly away, fly away bird
Why don't you listen to my words?

You're in great danger
Here comes the forest ranger.

So fly away birdie, so do look out
Make sure you see what's about.

Come back birdie another day
But come the other way!

Roqeeb Ajibola (11)
Loughborough Primary School, Brixton

Happiness

Happiness smells like beautiful roses,
It sounds like birds singing,
It looks like a new Lamborghini,
It tastes like a sweet strawberry,
It feels like flying an aeroplane.

Samuel Clayton
Loughborough Primary School, Brixton

Fear

Fear is like jumping off a roof,
It tastes like bitter blood,
Like being torn from limb to limb.
Fear is here.
Like being in a box,
It feels like dying.

Ryan Elliott (8)
Loughborough Primary School, Brixton

Stars

Stars . . .
Stars are shining
And glimmering in
The dark blue sky.
But when the sun
Rises up,
The stars fade away
In the sky.
When it's time
To go to bed
You see a full moon
And stars like a bed.
They're not just bundled
In one dark little space,
They are scattered everywhere,
So stars are light.

It is fun when you
Count the stars.
It is even fun when
They make pictures.
It's so much fun
When you are camping,
Looking at the stars.

Stars make you hungry
Because they remind
You of chocolate,
Milky Way or Maltesers.
Thinking of it melting,
Like Aeros popping here
And popping there.

Tian Wallace (10)
Loughborough Primary School, Brixton

Who U?

Who u? Who u?
In the bright daylight
Weeeeeeeeeeeeee
Go the little children
Down the slide.

Who u? Who u?
In the bright daylight
Waaaaaayyyyyyyyyy
Go the children on the swing
The children fly.

Who u? Who u?
In the bright daylight
Children run around
Around the park
Like birds.

Who u? Who u?
In the bright daylight
Wildlife circles
Their world
The children's playground.

Who u? Who u?
In the bright daylight
Children climb
In the jungle
On the trees.

Who u? Who u?
In the bright daylight
Round and round
Goes the merry-go-round
Round and round.

Kwadwo A Kyei (11)
Loughborough Primary School, Brixton

Loughborough Child

Behind you
Loughborough child
People you left behind

Around you
Loughborough child
People sad to see you go

Above you
Loughborough child
The Heaven praising you

Beside you
Loughborough child
Your friends and family proud

Think about your past
Your old and young friends

And new beginnings
Secondary school

Will things be all right?
At least friends will be there.

And you, oh Loughborough child
Think of your old teachers
Telling you not to forget them

And the very last hug
Be strong, be proud
And Loughborough
Tears falling down his face

And at secondary school
Phone them about your
Secondary adventure

Going to a big part of your life
Do your best with all your might.

Kane Nosworthy (11)
Loughborough Primary School, Brixton

Fear

Fear is black like a cave with darkness.
It feels like lava falling from the blue sky.
It sounds like everything is quiet.
It looks like the fearful sun throwing hot balls of fire.
It reminds me of someone punching a boy.
It tastes like hot pepper burning in your mouth.
It smells like burning houses.
It sounds like monsters caring people.
It looks like the sun is burning the world.

Michael Rodrigues (9)
Loughborough Primary School, Brixton

Sadness

Sadness is the colour green,
Like the boring old trees.
Sadness tastes like salt.
Sadness smells like the disgusting old sewers.
Sadness sounds like tears dropping.
Sadness reminds me of thunder and lightning clashing together.
Sadness feels like you want to cry your eyes out.

Hayley Gale
Loughborough Primary School, Brixton

Anger

The colour of anger is red like an exploding volcano.
Anger sounds like crashing, strong thunder.
Anger tastes like dirty dark blood.
Anger smells like rotten eggs and some dirty trash.
Anger feels like a crashing, strong tornado.
Anger looks like a hurricane full of madness.
Anger reminds me of Hell and my scariest nightmare.

Conard Haye (8)
Loughborough Primary School, Brixton

Happy Days

Let's go out,
I wonder what's there?
There could be a park or a city,
Flowers as blue as the sky,
Grass as green as a leaf,
Let's go out.

Let's go out,
Houses as white as paper,
Sun as bright as butter.
Let's go out.

Mariama Seydou (8)
Loughborough Primary School, Brixton

Anger!

Anger is orange like an erupting volcano.
It feels like red-hot coal.
It tastes so bitter.
It smells like a dirty river.
It sounds like thunder.

Stephanie Homawoo
Loughborough Primary School, Brixton

Love

Love is pink like sweet fluffy cotton candy
Love sounds like beautiful angels singing day and night
Love tastes like tasty ripe strawberries
Love smells like the best perfume in Heaven
Love feels like you are flying through the air
Love looks like a room made out of pure gold
Love reminds you of the best day of your whole life.

Diana Yusuf (8)
Loughborough Primary School, Brixton

Laureate

L ove poetry
A crostic, limerick, have fun with all
U nderstand the art of poetry
R hythmic words, rhythmic beat, keep the momentum with your feet
E njoy the poem, enjoy the art
A rtistic poems are such fun so when you read one don't you run
T umble, rumble are pairs of rhyme, make sure you keep the time
E njoy this poem like every other.

Dayana Herrera Rodriguez (10)
Loughborough Primary School, Brixton

Creepy Noises!

Fire ladder
Crashing thunder
Blowing curtains
Sheet ghosts
Slamming windows
Creaking stairs
Moving house
Banging doors
Petrified.

Rikaya Johnson
Loughborough Primary School, Brixton

Love

Love is yellow like a flower falling from your hair.
Love reminds me of someone dancing in the sky.
Love is red like strawberries, delicious shiny strawberries.
It reminds me of my mum singing me a funny song.
It feels warm.
It looks like burning hot fire.
It sounds like a beautiful song.

Mohammed Bouadina (9)
Loughborough Primary School, Brixton

Anger

Anger feels like grumbling in the ground
Anger looks like a black horrible monster
Anger reminds me of fighting somebody
Anger sounds like a powerful volcano bursting
Anger tastes like a sour fruit
Anger smells like a steam of smoke
Anger smells like flames of fire
Anger tastes like fire
Anger feels like a volcano ready to blow powerful like an earthquake
Anger looks like the powerful sun
Anger looks like the Devil
Anger looks like a huge big boulder
Anger feels like a bomb
Anger sounds like a massive storm
Anger tastes like the darkness
Anger smells like a dusty book
Anger tastes like madness
Anger sounds like thunder
Anger feels like a big ball of rock
Anger feels like spikes.

Hamza Arif (8)
Loughborough Primary School, Brixton

Anger

Anger is like red hot chilli
It tastes like red shiny lava
It tastes like a volcano exploding
It feels like hot burning sun
It reminds me of the volcano bursting out of the blue sea
It looks like a person is exploding in a fire
It looks like a volcano is exploding like a bomb
It reminds me of a volcano bursting
Anger is a mad thing to do
Anger makes my eyes look red like a fire
And my body look red like a thunderstorm cloud.

Ammar Akram (8)
Loughborough Primary School, Brixton

Emotions And Feelings

Fear

Fear is red, the colour of blood
I see it when I have a cut
If I see red I go mad
Then I feel drowsy and sad
This time I'm gone the red and blood
Soon it won't be mine
I'm going to leave, I'm going and going
I can't communicate even through this poem
I know I'll bleed by my thigh
And end up as cannibal pie
So this day I won't stay
Instead I'm going to be buried in hay

Love

Love is red like love hearts
You see it when romance starts
You smell sweet lavender flowers
And remember Cupid's powers
You are on top of the world
You go over the top
You sing R 'n' B and hip hop
You can't stop
Even in your dreams you sing with a mop.

Rashad Johnson (10)
Loughborough Primary School, Brixton

Anger

Anger is steam coming out of your head
Anger is two heads being banged together hard
Anger is a raging bull seeing red
Anger is stressed violence
Anger is alive
It is a temper that naturally erupts.

Sean Brown (10)
Loughborough Primary School, Brixton

The Feeling

Love
Is the colour of pink
And tweety birds flying.
It's as beautiful as a fragrant rose.
Love.

Fear
Is the colour of grey
And a monster on your back.
It's as ugly as a dying sun.
Fear.

Happiness
Is the colour of yellow
And the stars around you.
It's as pretty as a wondrous land.
Happiness.

Hate
Is the colour of red
And the Devil on you.
It's as hideous as a howling wolf.
Hate.

Anger
Is the colour of purple
And a twisted aura.
It's as wrong as a torn paper.
Anger.

Sadness
Is the colour of green
And a cloud on top of your head.
It's as sad as a person dead.
Sadness.

Layla Habarek (10)
Loughborough Primary School, Brixton

Love!

Love is like a bird
Singing his way through the air.
Love is something
That you'll never give away.
Love is something precious,
That it will stay in your heart.
Love is like a path,
It will never close its way.
Love brings people together.

Amani Alam (10)
Loughborough Primary School, Brixton

Cinderella

I'm standing on the stairs in the magnificent hall,
Wearing the dress I brought for the ball,
It's long and flowery, sparkling white,
My tiara of diamonds shines in the light.

At the bottom of the stairs you're waiting for me
And I gracefully float down for all to see,
You take my hand and touch my face,
You're the only one I notice in the expansive space.

We're now dancing in shadows of flickering light,
Holding each other close, holding each other tight,
Then you kiss my lips in a loving embrace.

Time stands still whilst we are together,
Feels so good, seems forever,
I look at the clock, it cannot be right,
But the bell starts to chime confirming midnight.

But there's no need to leave from the ball tonight,
I'll be with you, my prince, for the rest of our life.

Amy Hilton-Banks (9)
Penwortham Primary School, Streatham

The Homeless Man

I start to sing my favourite song,
Although it's out of tune.
I hope I get some money,
Now or very soon.

But it's never going
To come about,
And I will always
Have that doubt.

I disappear every day
And my heart starts to fade,
And I worry that
The place where I laid

Would be empty and unoccupied,
Gone and bare,
And what makes me more upset
Is that no one would care.

I want to be an athlete,
Running for the stars,
But I'm locked up in this world,
It's like I'm behind bars.

It will never help me, dreaming,
It's never going to come true,
I'm so cold and frightened,
I'm turning blue.

This is my life that will never change,
Please help me before I fade away completely.
Thank you,
Make a difference for me.

Ansha Mootoo (10)
Penwortham Primary School, Streatham

Receipt Poem

Organic pork sausage,
Perfect with my mash.
Baked beans
Smothered on my toast.
A really useful pink box
To keep my really useful things in.
Cadbury's Dream chocolate,
Great for sleepyheads.
Margherita pizza,
Great for my teacher.
Kingsmill crumpets
Crown wind trumpets.

Lucy Gregory (9)
Penwortham Primary School, Streatham

Riddles

I'm in cat but not in bat,
I'm in unicycle but not in sat,
I'm in purse, also in plum,
I'm in board but not in rum,
I'm in octopus, also in fox,
I'm in anchor but not in box,
I'm in road but not in load,
I'm in sowed, also in rowed.

What am I?

I'm in willow, also in wings,
I'm in house but not in sing,
I'm in ice, also in mice,
I'm in time but not in dice,
I'm in eggs, also in legs,

What am I?

Georgia Field (9)
Penwortham Primary School, Streatham

The Wind

Rustling through the wavy trees
Crisp as a cornflake
Making mini whirlpools of dust and rubbish
Trying to blow down everything in its path
Making me freeze from my head down to the tips of my toes
Waiting for this horrible feeling to end
Finally it stops
The trees have fallen
I hope that won't happen again.

The next day is sunny and bright, fresh and new
And everything is calm again
But the wind will be coming back for revenge
When it is sunny I'm happy and no one can get in my way
But when the wind comes back it will completely ruin my day.

Maia Forde (8)
Penwortham Primary School, Streatham

The Black Cat

There's the black cat,
Dark as night.
Small beady eyes
Shining bright.

There's the black cat
In the moonlight,
Ready to pounce
And give us a fright.

There's the black cat,
Dark as night,
Small beady eyes
Shining bright.

Bethany Monk-Lane (10)
Penwortham Primary School, Streatham

Butterfly

B eautiful, graceful and you feel so light
U nder the stars, your colours are so bright
T wisting and turning, for all to see
T rusting no one, to be sure you stay free
E very day you have fun playing in the park
R acing from flower to flower from light until dark
F loating around you seem so soft in the air
L ook, I have a clip just like you that I wear in my hair
Y ou fly away, beautiful butterfly, fly, fly, fly . . .

Hope Ferary (8)
Penwortham Primary School, Streatham

Colours

As red as a rose
As yellow as the sun
As pink as a pig
As black as the night sky
As brown as chocolate
As green as grass
As orange as Jupiter
As blue as the sky
As purple as grapes.

Shakira Reece (10)
Penwortham Primary School, Streatham

Football Poem

R ed is the colour
O f the best football team
O nly they have Rooney playing
N udging balls into goal
E very single game
Y es, red is the colour that Rooney wears.

Max Weller (8)
Penwortham Primary School, Streatham

My Big Brother

My big brother
Is such a big bother
I want to rub him out
And replace him with another.

He's such a pain,
I feel like whipping him with a cane.

He's got a big head
And a stinky bed,
When he gets frustrated,
His eyes go red.

He's so loud,
It feels like I'm going to pop.
I want to run out of the house
To the sweet shop.

He never shuts up,
I feel like squashing him into a teacup.

When he hurts me or calls me rude names,
I feel horrible pain.
When he's been mean,
I curl up with my teddy bear.

I want to roll him up into a ball
And roll him down the gallery hall.

At the end of the day we start to play
And take care of each other every day!

Tayeba Ahmed (10)
Penwortham Primary School, Streatham

Sun

S tifling and hot
U nder the sun
N oisy children running wild.

Rose Eaglesfield (10)
Penwortham Primary School, Streatham

The Four Seasons

Summer flowers growing high,
Summer sunshine in the sky.
Summer's coming, it's on its way,
The sun is out, come on let's play.

Winter chill and snowflakes falling
And Christmas on its way, it's coming.
Summer's gone and winter's here
And ev'rything is crystal clear.

Singing birds I hear in spring,
Tulips and lilies now I bring.
The falling leaves of autumn time,
Gold and red and brown and lime.

Autumn leaves are falling down
And the golden tips are like the point of a crown.
The leaves fall off with graceful care,
So they're leaving the trees completely bare.

So there you are, the four seasons are complete,
We never know what may happen next,
Whether it's autumn, or summer, or spring, or winter related,
The weather will change, but you can't make it.

Sèverine Howell-Meri (8)
Penwortham Primary School, Streatham

Horses

Horses really drive me wild,
Ever since I was a child.
I think horses are the best,
Wish I'd grown up in the west.
I'd be a cowgirl on my own
And ride a gorgeous strawberry roan.
I'd ride through woods and giant trees
And overtake the birds and bees.

Rachael Maybury (9)
Penwortham Primary School, Streatham

Caterpillar

C rawling
A gile
T ickly when on your hand
E legant
R apacious
P attering along
I nching
L ong
L eggy
A crobatic
R avenous.

Matilda Botsford (9)
Penwortham Primary School, Streatham

Riddle

Cleverer than all the scientists in the world
It can do almost anything
It works like a robot
It can play any tune
You can change the volume as quick as lightning
One click can change everything.

Answer: Computer.

Zoe Forester (9)
Penwortham Primary School, Streatham

My Rubber Duck

My rubber duck is so, so still
My rubber duck won't even eat a pill
My rubber duck is so safe and still
But when I squeeze him he squeals
He is very cuddly in the bath
And every time I see him he makes me laugh.

Ethan Sampson (8)
Penwortham Primary School, Streatham

Crazy Pets

I have a pet rabbit who thinks she's Snoopy,
At night she goes loopy.

I have a pet goldfish who eats a lot,
He's got a friend who is a dot.

I have a dog,
Who loves a frog.

I have a pet monkey who is very silly,
He's got a friend called Billy.

Hope James (9)
Penwortham Primary School, Streatham

Have A Guess

The first letter is in elephant and not in sand.
The second letter is in voice but not in quiet.
The third letter is in Emma but not in Sam.
The fourth letter is in record but not in case.
The fifth letter is in yesterday but not in tomorrow.
The sixth letter is in done but not in jam.
The seventh letter is in able but not in sound.
The eighth letter is in yellow but not in mum.
This word includes today.

Jiraporn Mcgill (9)
Penwortham Primary School, Streatham

Riddle Me This

I live in a doctor's room,
I am very, very hard,
I make parts of people statues,
Who am I?

A: Cast.

Jordan Hadfield (9)
Penwortham Primary School, Streatham

Nonsense Poem

The people in France
teach frogs' legs to dance
while the snails look on in a trance.

If you visit Brazil
you may need a pill
which is kept in a till.

When I went to Australia
my great aunt Azalea
painted her face like a dahlia.

When I lived in Spain
I saw a man get hit by a train
and somehow fell down the drain.

I have a friend farmer
who lived in the Bahamas
and also slipped on a banana.

Elliot Winspear (8)
Penwortham Primary School, Streatham

Guess Who?

I am climbing up a tree
Getting leaves as I pass by.
Moving slowly there isn't any here,
That's so awful, and then I give a sigh.

If anyone could guess
What this amazing creature could be
They would definitely come and see
The one, the only, me!

Guess who?

Panayiotis Koushi (9)
Penwortham Primary School, Streatham

My Dog Called Ben

I have a dog,
His name is Ben,
I've had him since
I don't know when.

I take him out
For a daily walk
And sometimes wish
That he could talk.

He's my best friend,
He's always about,
Even though
He makes me *shout*.

Chloe Corne (10)
Penwortham Primary School, Streatham

Stuart

Let me tell you about Stuart, my old friend
If you needed a fiver he would lend
He is so kind and thoughtful
His world is so colourful
He brings me lots of presents of 'Bratz'
And tells me about stupid facts
If I cry any tears
He says, 'Hey, have no fears'
I so love him that Stuart Obsorne
I wish he was my dad when I was born.

Antalia Delgado (9)
Penwortham Primary School, Streatham

Tregunc

I must go back to Tregunc,
Back to my bright cosy cottage,
Back to my favourite place in the world.

Back to my serene great garden,
With the sun glowing on my back,
Playing cards with my family,
Surely it's all I could wish for.

Cycling down a cool, shady path,
In the distance I can hear the waves,
Gracefully floating onto the soft sand,
On my way to the creek.

The blue waters mixing in
With the beautiful, swishing green seaweed,
Sitting on a rock drinking a cold Coke,
Watching lizards go by.

Grace Thomas (9)
Penwortham Primary School, Streatham

When I Went For A Walk In A Book

When I went for a walk in a book,
I touched a picture boy's leg and it shook.
The paper was hard to flip
And they kept on trying to nip.
Then I made friends with the paperboy
But the E kept saying I was a toy.
I started to argue with the G
'Cause he thought I was a flee.
I said I was only a kid
But I expected to see a lid.
The K didn't understand one word
So I liked to call him a bird.

Jules Bleckman (9)
Penwortham Primary School, Streatham

Right Now

Right now I feel angry
Right now I'm really mad
Right now I'm really frustrated
Right now I'm really sad

I feel angry about writing
I feel confused about my poem
I feel like running out to play
From this room, I feel like goin'.

Jake Seymour (10)
Penwortham Primary School, Streatham

Chocolate

C ream of caramel in my mouth
H ot chocolate bubbling in my mouth
O rganic cocoa beans growing in the ground
C elebrations sold at Christmas
O ccasionally we eat Heroes
L ion bars roaring in my mouth
A bubbling sensation all around
T iny Aeros in big packets
E normous Easter eggs in the shop.

Sophie Fox (9)
Penwortham Primary School, Streatham

Riddle Poem

It is a bar of an unusual kind,
Make some bubbles from its mind,
Mix some water, get bubbles galore,
After that you'll get some more.

I'm an everyday object,
What am I?

Natalie Maybury (9)
Penwortham Primary School, Streatham

Things I Like

Bright lights flashing
Sweaty players dashing
Crowds chanting Man United
Fans getting very excited

My favourite car's a Lamborghini
Because I've liked it since I was weenie
My dream is to fly
Way up in the sky

You can't see me come past
Because I'm so fast
I'm really funny
And I love money

I like going to my house
It's so quiet you can't even hear a mouse
I get into my bed
And rest my tired head.

Ben Bhogal (10)
Penwortham Primary School, Streatham

The Sophisticated Lady

I know a lady whose name is Kate
Who's really quite the sophisticate.
Who swishes round in flowing dresses
And wears her hair in curly tresses.
She loves to invite her friends for tea
But somehow never invites me.
They nibble on cucumber sandwiches
And talk a lot of different languages.
They retire to the garden for a game of croquet,
A perfect way to end the day.
So now you know about sophisticated Kate,
If she sends you an invite, please don't be late.

Chelsea Garwood (10)
Penwortham Primary School, Streatham

My Dreams

I like dreams
Good dreams
Bad dreams
And even
Sad dreams

Dreams I like
Scary dreams
Fairy dreams
And even
Sad dreams

I like dreams
Action dreams
True dreams
And that's
Why I like dreams

Good dreams
Bad dreams
And even
Sad dreams.

Zainab Malik (9)
Penwortham Primary School, Streatham

Troublesome Twins

I have a baby brother and sister who are twins
They always seem to scream and whinge.

They fight each other
And make more work for my mother.

My sister doesn't want to eat
And my brother has smelly feet!

They sometimes have crying fits
But I still love them to bits.

Nadia Ahmed (10)
Penwortham Primary School, Streatham

My Biography Poem

His name is Riyaaz and he loves sweet shops
He loves Man U but hates lid tops
He likes writing adventure stories
But hates learning literacy.

He used to live at Nimrod Road
And wishes his brother was a toad
He likes eating chocolate bars
And would never like to go to Mars.

His friends are Ben, Ramone, Adnan and lots of others
But wishes he had more brothers
He likes reading books
But hates to cook.

Riyaaz Patel (10)
Penwortham Primary School, Streatham

My Name Is Uzayr

My name is Uzayr
I am from Mauritius
And I always wash the dishes

I was born in 1997
And I am eleven
But I am afraid I will not go to Heaven

I want to go to Mauritius
Because it is the richest
And the crunchiest

My name is Uzayr
And some people call me the mayor

I like basketball
But not as much as I like football

I am Uzayr.

Uzayr Subratty (9)
Penwortham Primary School, Streatham

The Giraffe, The Pelly And Me

The pink and purple flower of the tinkle-tinkle tree,
Walnuts and salmon of course, yippee.

The patented beak and ever so long neck,
Mind you though Pelly might peck.

And Billy of course, the manager of the gang,
He's perfect in every way with no green blood or a fang.

Now they clean windows for the duke of Hampshire,
He's even got a clear view to see the pier.

Apples and cherries he grows,
Where he keeps them nobody knows.

'The grubber' they used for the window cleaning shop,
When young Billy saw that he got quite a shock.

That's the giraffe, the Pelly and me,
As you can see.

Ammara Khan (10)
Penwortham Primary School, Streatham

Feelings

Feelings can feel happy,
Feelings can feel mad,
Feelings can feel crazy,
Feelings can feel bad.

Feelings can feel weird,
Feelings can feel dazed,
Feelings can feel used,
Feelings can feel amazed.

Feelings can feel shocked,
Feelings can feel glad,
Feelings can feel angry,
Feelings can feel sad.

Aisling Towl (10)
Penwortham Primary School, Streatham

Crazy Pets

I have a pet dog, his name is Billy,
He has curly hair and is always really silly.

My pet's called Max, he is a nice cat,
Every time he eats he gets a bit fat.

I have a pet rabbit, he has a big hat,
One day he went outside and ate a big bat.

My pet's called Gold, she is a goldfish,
She likes to eat in a very big dish.

I have a pet guinea pig, his name is Stig,
He eats a lot of food and likes to chew a twig.

Hamza Mahmood (9)
Penwortham Primary School, Streatham

Anger!

Anger is when you blurt things out
Things you don't want to say
Anger can be a bit of jealousy
And you hope it just won't stay

Anger can make your body burn up
Like a house catching on fire
Anger is a horrible feeling
And you feel like you can bend wire

Anger is when you feel evil
And want to really hurt someone
Anger is when you're annoyed and upset
And you can't have any fun.

Alice Edmundson (9)
Penwortham Primary School, Streatham

Wave

A curling creature
A manky monster
A foamy fighter
A silver soldier
A diving dolphin
A crawling crab
A slithering snake
A cunning killer
A deathly thing
A wave.

Megan Barratt (10)
Penwortham Primary School, Streatham

I Am Poem

I am silly,
I am funny,
I wonder if I will get a job.
I hear an electric guitar,
I hear George Galloway shouting at the newsman,
I want loads of sweets from the sweet shop,
I am silly,
I am funny.

Hasan Gaffar (10)
Penwortham Primary School, Streatham

Wind - Haiku

The wind blew me back
It came from the dark north-east
Where my friend's house is.

Alana Emery (8)
Robin Hood Primary School, Kingston Upon Thames

Promise Of Friendship

I want to be friends with you,
Till the sea is green,
Till cats chase dogs
And monsters roam the Earth.

If we are friends
I will lend you my extra special
Real silver charm bracelet
And stand up for you when you need me.

I will give you
The bravery of a lion's roar
The magic of dreams
And a glowing pearl.

I will like you more than
A beautiful blood-red rose
A triple fudge ice cream
And the golden burning sun.

Dyna Tlemsani (11)
Robin Hood Primary School, Kingston Upon Thames

I Hate . . . I Love

I hate the horrendous voice of Michael Jackson
But I love the fast way he moves.

I hate the yucky taste of pizza
But I love the way it is crispy around the edge.

I hate the thought of messy art
But I love the way I get dirty.

I hate the smell of fish oil
But I love the way that it drips onto the spoon.

I hate the sound of someone vomiting
But I love the way it spreads on the floor.

Natalia Goncalves (11)
Robin Hood Primary School, Kingston Upon Thames

Promise Of Friendship

I want to be friends with you
Till the Earth stops spinning,
Till I stop singing
And until elephants fly.

If we are friends
I will jump over the moon
And share everything with you.

I will give you the stars at night
The key to Davy Jones' locker
And a shoulder to lean on
When you need it.

I will like you more than
My favourite teddy bear
And the nervous feeling in my tummy
When I am about to go on a roller coaster.

Amber Pearce-Debono (10)
Robin Hood Primary School, Kingston Upon Thames

I Hate, I Love

I hate the plain taste of shepherd's pie
But I love the smoothness of the creamy topping.

I hate the sound of people scratching the blackboard
But I love the way you can smudge the chalk.

I hate the mouldy smell of bin bags
But I love the way they rip easily.

I hate the vomiting smell of fish
But I love the way the scary eyes stare at you.

I hate the taste of hot caramel
But I love it when it drips off the spoon.

I hate the coldness of snow
But I love throwing snowballs.

Nikki Whitby (11)
Robin Hood Primary School, Kingston Upon Thames

Promise Of Friendship

I want to be friends with you
Till the gods' hearts stop beating,
Till elephants can talk Chinese
And pigs fly.

If we are friends
I will give you my Bob Charlton signature
And I will do your maths homework for you.

I will give you a shining star
From the heart of the universe,
The heat of the sun,
The first breath of a newborn baby
And the beat of my heart.

I will like you more than
The Wembley Stadium,
The plasma television
And the day I leave school.

Nathan Richardson (11)
Robin Hood Primary School, Kingston Upon Thames

I Hate . . . I Love

I hate the boring sound of classical music
But I love the way it keeps my nan entertained.

I hate the paleness of sausages before they are cooked
But I love their sharp taste.

I hate the moody ways of Simon Cowell
But I love his big house.

I hate the black colour of bin bags
But I love the way that they keep litter in them.

I hate the taste of fattening doughnuts
But I love the patterns on them.

I hate the way strawberries get squashed
But I love the tasty juice!

Bonnie Maclaren (11)
Robin Hood Primary School, Kingston Upon Thames

Promise Of Friendship

I want to be friends with you
Till Pluto crashes into the Earth,
Till Mickey Mouse comes to life
And I turn into a frog.

If we are friends
I will lend you my science encyclopaedia
And I will give you my X-Files DVD.

I will give you the light of a Supernova,
The life of all living organisms,
A trip around all the dimensions
And my digital camera.

I will like you more than
The Internet,
The feeling of breaking the sound barrier
And me seeing extraterrestrial life forms
Flying in the sky.

Daniel Knowles (11)
Robin Hood Primary School, Kingston Upon Thames

Excuses, Excuses!

'Why are you late for school?'
'I travelled through time.
It was fun, I met Adolph Hitler.'
'Where's your homework boy?'
'Umm, a bulldog from next door ate it Sir!'
'What like the time when a duck ate it?'
'Not that bad Sir.'
'Oh! OK class line up for music.'
'Sorry Sir I haven't got my guitar Sir.'
'Where it is?'
'A mouse chewed the strings Sir.'
'Right, that's the cane for you boy!'

Alexandra Jellye (10)
Robin Hood Primary School, Kingston Upon Thames

What Is Human Life But A Game Of Cricket!

What is human life but a game of cricket!
It's a great creation, a great game,
With its skill, strategy, talent and beauty,
It's a touch of magic from God,
It's the shine in my eye and a corner in my smile.

Whenever the ball hits the stumps,
A great cheer comes out
And the bowler gets pride and relief.
Whenever the ball goes past those ropes,
A great cheer comes out
And the batsman gets pride and confidence.

So what is human life but a game of cricket!

Zan Mahmood (10)
Robin Hood Primary School, Kingston Upon Thames

Promise Of Friendship

I want to be friends with you
Till the Earth stops spinning,
Till birds stop flying
And dinosaurs walk the Earth again.

If we are friends
I will give you my diamonds
And I will do your homework.

I will give you all the money in the world,
The petals from the finest rose,
A box with all the stars in the galaxy
And a feather from the firebird.

I will like you more than
The first laugh of a baby,
The sound of the rushing sea
And the last roar of a lion.

Craig Norris (10)
Robin Hood Primary School, Kingston Upon Thames

Summer

The wind is as hot as an exploding fire,
Swerving waters skid through the refreshing reefs as a curving
                                        soccer sphere,
Swiftly as a rabbit the soft, silky, smooth sand swishes and splashes.
The blazing hot ball is a striking sun.
Picnics smell of succulent sandwiches and fresh summer fruits.
The air is calm, the wind is cool, the humans have arrived.
Splash, splash, splash, the glorious swimming pools have erupted.

A spot of golf is around the corner,
Tiger Woods hits with an 8-inch iron and a smack,
It swerves, right to left.

The summer is at an end, the wind is back,
The end is near . . .

Sunny Ratilal (10)
Robin Hood Primary School, Kingston Upon Thames

Promise Of Friendship

I want to be friends with you
Till the moon drops,
Till there is no love in the world
And until all animals are extinct.

If we are friends
I will lend you my games
And I will give you my last piece of chocolate.

I will give you the twinkle from the last star in the galaxy,
The brightness of a sunray,
An everlasting gobstopper
And a footprint from the last walking dinosaur.

I will like you more than
The latest PSP game I bought,
The brightness in your eyes
And the first sight of the sun rising.

Carl Mayes (10)
Robin Hood Primary School, Kingston Upon Thames

Snow - Haiku

The snow is coming
The weather is nice and cold
The snow has stopped now.

Reece Xavier (8)
Robin Hood Primary School, Kingston Upon Thames

Rain - Haiku

The rain is falling
I like the rain, it is cold
There is lots of rain.

Zaynab Osman (8)
Robin Hood Primary School, Kingston Upon Thames

The Snow - Haiku

It is snowing now
It is so sunny and hot
It is raining now.

Kane Corby (8)
Robin Hood Primary School, Kingston Upon Thames

Sun - Haiku

The sun is shining
It's shining on flowerpots
Shining on the pond.

Britney Reilly (7)
Robin Hood Primary School, Kingston Upon Thames

Rain - Haiku

It is raining now
Raindrops on my window ledge
When will the rain stop?

Justin Le (8)
Robin Hood Primary School, Kingston Upon Thames

Autumn - Haiku

Autumn has conkers
Conkers are cool, very cool
Conkers are so hard.

Nathanael Taylor (8)
Robin Hood Primary School, Kingston Upon Thames

Weather - Haiku

The rain is falling
Leaves are floating steadily
Spring will come soon now.

Erin Ailes (8)
Robin Hood Primary School, Kingston Upon Thames

The Snow - Haiku

The snow is shiny
and it falls down from the dark
and it falls down now.

Hassan Mustafa (8)
Robin Hood Primary School, Kingston Upon Thames

In A Perfect World

In a perfect world
we would share and care for each other
One day we will all die and fly to Heaven
and some poor child dies at the age of seven
In other countries they are suffering of diseases
and here we think sneezes are bad
In this country we are really greedy
and people in Africa are really needy.

Tommy Iqbal (10)
Robin Hood Primary School, Kingston Upon Thames

Me And My Friends

My friends and I like to play,
Or sit around talking all day.
But what we usually do
Is skip around
The playground,
But with two ropes not one
And that's how we have some fun.

Nora Hakim (9)
Robin Hood Primary School, Kingston Upon Thames

The Spiral

A spiral is round and it looks like an eye.
It can hypnotise you if it wants to.
It gets smaller and smaller when it gets to the middle.
It's like a wave in the sea going up and down
And when it splashes it goes everywhere
And this is a poem about spirals.

Antonella Posteraro (10)
Robin Hood Primary School, Kingston Upon Thames\

Snow Leopards

Snow leopards are as white as snow
And as soft as a pillow
Snow leopards are as gentle as can be
And as strong as a grizzly bear.

Daniel McQue (10)
Robin Hood Primary School, Kingston Upon Thames

The Moon

The moon rises like a golf ball being hit into the air.
The moon is a big silver star.
The moon is like a big clock telling us to sleep or not.
The moon is a face which is crying.

Joshua Davis (10)
Robin Hood Primary School, Kingston Upon Thames

Colours In The Sky

Sky-blue will brighten the sky in the morning.
Yellow will make the sun stand out.
Grey will get the sun running and the rain pouring.
While sunset-red will get a lovely sight.

Fatima Hussien (9)
Robin Hood Primary School, Kingston Upon Thames

My Star - Haiku

Little star smiling
in the shining sky at night
with love up above.

Mollie Cummings (9)
Robin Hood Primary School, Kingston Upon Thames

The Writer Of This Poem
(Inspired by 'The Writer of this Poem' by Roger McGough)

The writer of this poem
Is as creamy as a cake
As wicked as a witch
As wild as a buffalo.

The writer of this poem
Is as light as a feather
As crazy as a monkey
As cheeky as a squirrel.

The writer of this poem
Is as hot as a dragon
As huge as a house
As scary as a mouse
(if you're an elephant.)

Isla Paterson (9)
Robin Hood Primary School, Kingston Upon Thames

The Tiger

A proud creature,
Black and orange stripes,
He's big and bold,
Muscly and fast.

Eyes like headlights,
Claws like knives,
Whiskers like ropes,
Hair like wires.

The handsome tiger,
Still walks today,
But will he walk tomorrow?

Eloise Emery (10)
Robin Hood Primary School, Kingston Upon Thames

The Writer Of This Poem
(Inspired by 'The Writer of this Poem' by Roger McGough)

The writer of this poem
Is as wild as a monkey,
As fast as a squirrel,
As evil as a devil.

The writer of this poem
Is as strong as a bee,
As slimy as a slug,
As bonkers as a conker.

The writer of this poem
Is as creamy as a cake,
As cool as a dragon,
As cheeky as a monkey.

Amber Russell (9)
Robin Hood Primary School, Kingston Upon Thames

Sun - Haiku

Sun, how bright you shine
You look pretty nice up there
Your shine is so nice.

Alana Blackwell-Barnett (7)
Robin Hood Primary School, Kingston Upon Thames

Cat - Haiku

Cats are very cuddly
They nuzzle you to stroke them
Sleeping on your lap.

Rebekah Smith (7)
Robin Hood Primary School, Kingston Upon Thames

My Magic Box
(Based on 'Magic Box' by Kit Wright)

I will put in my box . . .
Snow from the mountain tops,
The nine planets in space
And a picture of my loving mum.

I will put in my box . . .
A part of the pretty moon,
A piece of paradise
And the whistle of the wind.

I will put in my box . . .
The smile of the sun,
The happiness of the moon
And the twinkle and sparkle of the stars.

My box is fashioned from
Burning fire
From a dying dragon,
Its hinges are made from
Sharp dragons' teeth.

In my box I will sail
The seven seas
And go to places I have never been,
This is a real adventure.

Andrew O'Neill (11)
Robin Hood Primary School, Kingston Upon Thames

I Wish You Enough

I wish you enough to die so you can come in peace
I also wish crime so you can call the police
I really wish you badness so you can really give
I wish you lots of killing so you can live
I wish you the truth so you can tell lies
I wish you enough hellos to face goodbyes.

Naomi Arkaah (10)
Robin Hood Primary School, Kingston Upon Thames

My Magic Box
(Based on 'Magic Box' by Kit Wright)

I will put in my box . . .
The deadly fang of a snake,
The head of a wolf
And the smoke from a dragon's nose.

I will put in my box . . .
The tail of a comet,
The pointy fin from a shark
And a rock from the moon.

I will put in my box . . .
The wild wind from a hurricane,
The fire from a volcano
And the hair from a lion.

My box is fashioned from the waves
And the corners are shiny crystals
Made by the gods.

In my box I will fly in a hurricane
Like a bird in the night sky.

Ali Mustafa (10)
Robin Hood Primary School, Kingston Upon Thames

The Wolf

I am as strong as a lion,
I appear at night,
I am as tough as a boxer,
I scare the fright.

I howl so loud, I can be heard for miles around.
I am the best and that will never die out,
I am the predator never to be forgotten.

Sharif Dougramaji (10)
Robin Hood Primary School, Kingston Upon Thames

My Magic Box
(Based on 'Magic Box' by Kit Wright)

I will put in my box . . .
The sound of a baby dolphin,
A witch's book of spells
And a crystal clear smile from my loving mum.

I will put in my box . . .
A baby's first laugh,
A whisper from a shooting star
And a misty cloud covering the moon.

I will put in my box . . .
A pillow for my tears when I cry,
A secret only for two
And an everlasting hug.

My box is fashioned from
Shiny silver stars in the night sky
With ruby red hearts
And glitter clouds all over.
At last in the corners are dreams to come true.

I shall keep my magic box
Forever and ever and ever.

Ellie Macnamara (11)
Robin Hood Primary School, Kingston Upon Thames

Antonia Autumn

She brings the leaves down,
Safely to the ground.
And the wind clouds start to tune in,
The flowers die and say goodbye.

The clouds turn grey
And butterflies pray that summer will soon be here.
But yet the leaves are still to be red
And couples are still to be wed.

Isabel Slatter (10)
Robin Hood Primary School, Kingston Upon Thames

The Writer Of This Poem
(Inspired by 'The Writer of this Poem' by Roger McGough)

The writer of this poem
Is taller than an elephant
As strong as a bear
As clever as a scientist.

The writer of this poem
Is faster than a cheetah
As clean as a fish
As sharp as a pen.

Dominique Campbell (8)
Robin Hood Primary School, Kingston Upon Thames

Love

Love, love, love
is like a dove
flying in the air
with love and care.

Arguments and fights
with lots of knights
trusted and treated
just as you greeted.

Work, work, work
don't be a jerk
pick up the phone
and don't moan and groan.

The heart is red
and when it's kept
you'll feel proud
and speak so loud.

Butterflies in your tummy
that's not very yummy
a good expert you will be
you will see how great you will see.

Daniel Spinola (10)
St Joseph's RC Primary School, Chelsea

Sadness

Sad is grey on a dull winter's day,
Sad sounds like babies crying,
Sad feels like a little girl very cold.

Going to a funeral,
Attic being destroyed,
Someone being violent,
I feel sad when I get annoyed.

Sad tastes like melted ice cream,
Sad reminds you of fish fingers being burnt,
Sad smells of a room, no one has been in it.

Going to a funeral,
Attic being destroyed,
Someone being violent,
I feel sad when I get annoyed.

Mia Dalimot (8)
St Joseph's RC Primary School, Chelsea

Happiness

Happiness means love and joy,
When a child is squishing a lovely toy,
Children play, church bells ringing
And the choir's happily singing.

Happiness means hope of love,
As a baby looks up above,
Babies sleep, sweetly peek
And the baby happily being cheeky.

Happiness means royal love,
Like a joyful dove flying above,
Loving kisses, joyful mums
And a hug from up above.

Paula Vilelas (9)
St Joseph's RC Primary School, Chelsea

Fury

Sirens ringing in your ear,
Steam trains screech as they pull into the station,
The smoke of a cigarette which hasn't been put out,
The smell of pepper makes me sneeze,
Then I see red all around.
Tornado's darkness and bitterness from a friend,
The taste of chilli never seems to end,
Anger is a feeling you will never escape.

Daniela Santos (9)
St Joseph's RC Primary School, Chelsea

Happiness

When I'm happy I feel chatty,
When I'm happy I feel tappy,
When I'm happy I feel clappy,
When I'm happy I feel zappy.
O, feelings are everywhere,
Feelings go here and there,
Feelings go here and everywhere,
I give feelings lots of care.

Anais Espinosa (8)
St Joseph's RC Primary School, Chelsea

Happiness

Happiness is condensed milk with strawberries.
Happiness feels like the best day of your life.
Happiness sounds like violins and cellos.
Happiness reminds you of visiting your country.

Julio Mendes Santos (8)
St Joseph's RC Primary School, Chelsea

Hunger, Hate And Darkness

Hunger, hunger reminds me of smoke,
being hungry is no joke,
hunger is a flesh-ripping scavenger,
sharp teeth and bones he has no manager.

Hate reminds me of bloodthirsty sharks,
not giving up like when a dog barks,
when they smell blood they think of hate.

Darkness is very petrifying,
like every second you're hearing something dying,
when there's darkness things tend to be sleepy,
when sleeping in the open it seems very creepy.

Darkness is pitch-black and worrying,
from darkness everything is scurrying,
like getting stung by a thousand stinging nettles,
being in darkness is a real test of your mettle.

Hate is a non-forgiving feeling,
like that anger you get when you're screaming,
hate is a gloomy red,
hate is when you wish you were dead.

Hunger is grey, burnt and damp,
it feels like your belly is jumping off a ramp,
hunger has an emptiness about it,
being hungry isn't a good habit.

Darkness has a cold metal scent,
it smells like sleeping in a tent,
darkness smells like trees,
darkness is getting stung by bees.

Samuel Makanjuola (10)
St Joseph's RC Primary School, Chelsea

Fear

Fear is in your spirit
It tastes like blood from a spider
It sounds like nails on a blackboard
It's a grey fuzzy colour
Its smell is like a dead wolf
It reminds me of a witch killing people with her nails
It feels like you are being stretched apart
It sounds like footsteps coming out of nowhere
It looks like a dinosaur opening his mouth
with blood all over his teeth.

Dion Galligan (10)
St Joseph's RC Primary School, Chelsea

Anger

Anger is a dark roaring lion, thunder in the sky
A screaming dragon, screeching steam train
Kicking and punching and chilli peppers,
Anger is dark like a raging tornado with hot boiling water
Sea salt burning my tongue
Police siren getting a robber from stealing something
Anger is red when you cut yourself.

Lorena Perez (9)
St Joseph's RC Primary School, Chelsea

Hunger

Hunger is a black animal who is waiting for you to come out.
It reminds me of a dragon spitting fire at me.
It sounds like a wolf howling for his life
And waiting there to eat you up and even your bones.

Anthony Oliveira (10)
St Joseph's RC Primary School, Chelsea

Fun

It reminds me of people partying 24/7
Just like being in Heaven
Red faces, people always screaming
If you lose your voice there's always a person healing.

Thank you for these wonderful places
People are running like horses
All around the world
There are always funfairs being held.

I feel brave going on scary rides
Because the rides are all super high
On the rides you can always hear shouting
People normally counting -1, 2, 3, it feels like going down a mountain.

It tastes like salty sweat
Just when you see somebody you met
When your mother buys you a sweet from the shop
She's always protecting you like a cap.

Martin Alban (10)
St Joseph's RC Primary School, Chelsea

Happiness

Happiness is like having lots of treats,
maybe some cookies and little sweets.

Happiness is like thinking there are bright colours everywhere,
but please don't take them away, don't you dare.

It has a nice smell of biscuits being baked
and a lovely cocktail being shaked.

Happiness makes me feel like I am on a roller coaster ride
and knowing my friends are just by my side.

Happiness is like eating a piece of cake
especially a Victoria sponge that my nan can bake.

Happiness is as bright as the sun shining
and as joyful as doing lots of rhyming.

Rosie Bennett (9)
St Joseph's RC Primary School, Chelsea

Laughter

Laughter reminds me of fun,
things like funfairs and clowns.
Giggling tastes like lollies
and sherbet, sweets and wine gums.

It sounds like a hyena
laughing out loud,
looks like happiness
and excitement.

The colour of laughter
is bright pink, sky-blue,
grass-green, purple
and even the hues of the sun.

Laughter comes
from your mouth and tummy,
everyone needs to laugh,
so laughter comes from the world.

Serena Tavares Firmino (10)
St Joseph's RC Primary School, Chelsea

Darkness

The location of this dark place is in a dark, dark cave
The taste of this horrid place is the dangerous underground of the ancient tombs.

The stench of this place is like in nightclubs
The colour is a thick black.

It sounds like a hurricane rapidly going through Australia
It feels like a thousand knives stabbing you through the chest.

It reminds me of getting trapped in a coffin
It looks like space with no stars.

It feels like a big cactus
It tastes like a rotten apple.

William Ruales (9)
St Joseph's RC Primary School, Chelsea

Fun

Fun has a taste like candyfloss, sponge cake, sweets and chocolate.
Fun has a smell like cookies just come out of a brand new oven.
Fun has beautiful colours like pink, light green, yellow and baby-blue.
Fun looks like crazy Year 2 children running around on a playground
on a refreshing sunny, hot day with some ice cream.
Fun has a loveable feeling like flying in the air
and feeling the soft wind pushing against you.
Fun is in a circus full of people that are enjoying themselves
and laughing.
Fun is in a funfair full of people and fabulous rides.
Fun wonderfully sounds like children shouting as loud as a whistle
on a tall building.
Fun excitedly reminds me of myself when I was younger playing
with my friends and myself with my family going to a funfair.

Kari-Ann De Sa Da Silva (10)
St Joseph's RC Primary School, Chelsea

Happiness

It feels like babies
And love
Fun and cool
Yellow or orange, blue, violet, pink, red
It sounds like happy people playing
Inside of people
It feels loving
You can't see it but you can feel it
You can imagine it
It is nice
You can't breath it
It makes you excited
It makes you laugh
It is so joyful.

Adriana Camacho (10)
St Joseph's RC Primary School, Chelsea

Fun

Fun is a tingling like a spider crawling up you
It makes me laugh
It looks joyful and colourful and makes you go a bit mad and crazy.
It makes your imagination really go cuckoo
There are lots of colours a bit like the rainbow -
yellow, orange, pink, blue, purple
It smells like fresh air and like spring.
It sounds like lots of people jumping around and laughing.

Alana Barker-Perez (10)
St Joseph's RC Primary School, Chelsea

Silence

Silence is quiet and dark,
It smells like smoke and plants,
Looks still and frightening,
You find it everywhere that it quiet,
Reminding you of being alone in a graveyard,
White, grey and turquoise,
Feeling lonely and alone in the world,
Wishing you had someone to talk to.

Alison Martinez (10)
St Joseph's RC Primary School, Chelsea

Anger

Anger is mixed with all different colours.
Some colours are red, some colours are orange.
It reminds me of people who keep on annoying
And some friends that keep destroying.
It smells like fire and smoke
And maybe something just burnt.

Leon Xavier (10)
St Joseph's RC Primary School, Chelsea

Love

Love starts with kisses and hugs
Give your true love loveable mugs
Love in the air
Goes everywhere

Roses, flowers, incredible sensations
It goes around in all the nations
Romantic dinners go with wine
Which makes everything just divine

Flowers with cards travel around
With just a little giggle and sound
Charming, beautiful people are
Men with just amazing cars

God's favourite thing is love
He symbolises with a dove
When doves fly it's so smooth
It's almost as it does not move.

Rania Habib (10)
St Joseph's RC Primary School, Chelsea

When I'm Happy

When I'm happy I hear birds singing, children laughing
and a lullaby in my ear.
When I'm happy I feel feathers tickling me that makes me laugh
and I know birds are near.
When I'm happy I taste candyfloss and semi-skimmed milk
then that's when I have no fear.
When I am happy it reminds me of the yellow sunflowers
in the sunny field, being tickled and my mum saying, 'Hello dear!'
When I'm happy I smell flowers that smell like perfume,
a yummy strawberry and a green soft pear.

Jasmine De La Cruz (9)
St Joseph's RC Primary School, Chelsea

Darkness

Darkness is a damp rotting smell
It is a smell that really repels
As soon as you smell it the smell makes you want to be sick
Very quick like a flick of a tick

Like a hyena scavenging for a rotting animal
On a hot day eating as its name's a cannibal
Oozing blood dripping off its teeth
Birds sitting scarcely on some leaves

Darkness is misty clouds going over the moon
The colour is a blood-red maroon
Clouds that travel in scary formations
Terrorising people across all of the nations

It sounds like nails screeching on a blackboard
Or like thick gloop being poured
Even a horrible ghostly tune
Or like on a game hearing *doom!*

The feeling is cold and weary
It feels like someone has put me in a trance that is not the type
                              that is cheery
It feels like petals falling to the ground
Floating sadly all around

Darkness lives in hospitals where illness is passed around
Germs float freely, silently and crawl along the ground
The people there are grey and sad
And eventually they are driven mad

Darkness is in the church and with its people
It is passed around by silence in the steeple
The dark corners that are loaded in history
Everyone knows they hold so much mystery

Darkness is the blood that dripped from Jesus' head
The worst thing to happen was that Jesus was dead
His cross of death He had to hold
And left the world feeling cold.

Kace Bartley (9)
St Joseph's RC Primary School, Chelsea

What Is Darkness?

What is darkness?
When the light switches off it becomes dark
Darkness is like the African black panther
Darkness is like when we near the campfire
Darkness is like chocolate, rich and can be hard
Darkness sounds like animals scavenging for food at night
Darkness is like something you can't touch
Darkness is like a pattern
Darkness is a thing you can't hear
Darkness is like smoke.

James Poots (10)
St Joseph's RC Primary School, Chelsea

Romance

Love's best taste is of chocolate and wine,
Like red roses just so nice,
Chocolate pudding in your mind,
Heart-beating butterflies in your tummy,
The sweet, sweet taste of strawberry and golden honey,
Sweet-smelling roses,
Perfume floating in the summer breeze,
Wedding bells ringing,
The choir singing in that sunny cool breeze.

Fabio Nobrega (9)
St Joseph's RC Primary School, Chelsea

Sad

I feel sad when I am bad.
I feel sad when I hear a scary sound.
I feel sad when I am lonely.
I feel sad when my brother hits me.
I feel sad when I drink lemon juice.
I feel sad when I eat something sour.

Jessica Mendes (7)
St Joseph's RC Primary School, Chelsea

Loneliness

Loneliness can be found in a cold empty room,
in a dark strange cave next to a damp forest.
The sound of loneliness is like a scared hungry wolf,
looking for is pack in a pitch-black forest,
a cub all alone in the African desert crying out to its mother.

The colour of loneliness is a pale grey like the heavy clouds
                                                in the freezing winter,
it is a faint yellow like a person's face when shocked.
Loneliness tastes like dust from an old wrecked house,
a bitter and sour meat with no healthiness.

The smell of loneliness is like burnt ashes after a fire ran through
                                                a forest burning everything in its path,
it smells like dry dust in the busy streets of Pakistan.
The smell is a dead rotting rose given by a loved one
                                                who passed away,
it smells like strong killing smoke from a house which had caught fire.

Loneliness looks like a grey sky in the blackness of London
                                                in the winter.
Loneliness reminds me of a tree all alone on the hill and other trees
                                                all together on the other side of the hill
and a child playing on her own and other children playing together.

Marina Ayub (9)
St Joseph's RC Primary School, Chelsea

Sadness

Sadness is a colour grey that reminds you of an old woman's shawl.
Sadness sounds like moaning, wailing and whining.
Sadness feels like people lonely, upset and crying.
Plants dying, leaves falling to the ground,
Long winter nights all around.
Cold fish and chips, soggy ice cream,
Empty chocolate wrappers, raindrops falling in your dreams.

Daniela Silva (9)
St Joseph's RC Primary School, Chelsea

Fury

In my ears I can hear trumpets blasting loudly.
I can smell lots of unpleasant smells like my favourite meal
was just burnt.
It tastes like vinegar, lemons and lime all in one.
I can taste the bitterness of jealousy spreading on my tongue,
Reminding me of the exploding volcano
and the red fury spreading everywhere it can.
It makes me feel like I'm going to explode
because of the fire that is burning me inside.

Catarina Santos Moreira (9)
St Joseph's RC Primary School, Chelsea

Anger

Anger is in your brain,
passing through memory lane.

It tastes like heat
from the meat
in the street.

It feels like a ball of fire
that never expires.

It reminds me of war
in all the countries there is more and more.

A scream from the kettle
while listening to heavy metal.

The colour is red, orange, yellow and blue
from the candle that I aspire.

It smells like steam
from an electric beam.

Lorenzo Benavente (9)
St Joseph's RC Primary School, Chelsea

Happiness

Happiness is when chicks pop out of their eggs.
Happiness feels like doves flying in the breeze.
Fudge chocolate cake, creamy ice cream and strawberries'
green leaves.
It reminds me of babies born with red, red cheeks.
It smells of candles when Jesus rose!
Starfish, sunflowers and chicks are happiness.
Happiness is when you lie in the hot, hot sun.
Happiness is love and joy.

Mafalda Ribeiro (8)
St Joseph's RC Primary School, Chelsea

Young Writers Information

We hope you have enjoyed reading this book - and that you will continue to enjoy it in the coming years.

If you like reading and writing poetry drop us a line, or give us a call, and we'll send you a free information pack.

Alternatively if you would like to order further copies of this book or any of our other titles, then please give us a call or log onto our website at
www.youngwriters.co.uk

**Young Writers Information
Remus House
Coltsfoot Drive
Peterborough
PE2 9JX
(01733) 890066**